Emotional Intelligence at Work

Emotional Intelligence at Work

The Untapped Edge for Success

Hendrie Weisinger, Ph.D.

Jossey-Bass Publishers
San Francisco

Substantial discounts on bulk quantities of Jossey-Bass books are available to corporations, professional associations, and other organizations. For details and discount information, contact the special sales department at Jossey-Bass Inc., Publishers (415) 433-1740; Fax (800) 605-2665.

For sales outside the United States, please contact your local Simon & Schuster International Office.

Jossey-Bass Web address: http://www.josseybass.com

 Manufactured in the United States of America on Lyons Falls Turin Book. This paper is acid-free and 100 percent totally chlorine-free.

Library of Congress Cataloging-in-Publication Data

Weisinger, Hendrie.
    Emotional intelligence at work : the untapped edge for success /
Hendrie Weisinger. — 1st ed.
       p. cm.
    Includes bibliographical references and index.
    ISBN 0-7879-0952-1 (cloth : alk. paper)
       1. Psychology, Industrial. 2. Interpersonal relations. 3. Self-perception.
4. Emotions. I. Title.
HF5548.8.W433   1998
650.1'3—dc21
                                           97-21220
                                          CIP

FIRST EDITION
HB Printing 10 9 8 7 6 5 4 3 2

Contents

The Author

Hendrie Weisinger is a licensed psychologist with extensive experience in clinical, counseling, and organizational psychology. He teaches in executive education programs at universities across the United States and is a consultant to worldwide Fortune 500 companies, government agencies, educational systems, and mental health organizations. He is a leading authority on the application of emotional intelligence, an expert in anger management, the originator of the highly regarded techniques of Criticism Training, and the author of several successful books. He has appeared on hundreds of television and radio shows, including "Donahue," "Oprah," "Good Morning America," and "The Today Show."

Acknowledgments

There are many people to acknowledge. First, Larry Alexander recognized the importance of emotional intelligence at work. He got the ball rolling by bringing the book to Jossey-Bass. Next is Susan Williams, who skillfully blended emotional intelligence into her manuscript critique. She saw exactly what the book needed and showed excellent judgment by bringing in Karen Sharpe as developmental editor. Karen did an outstanding job. I have no doubt that this book is far superior because of her writing and editorial talents.

Next is John Mayer. John generously shared with me his knowledge on emotional intelligence; his articles on the subject were my key theoretical resources. Credit should also be given to his colleague, Peter Salovey.

I want to recognize a number of business school executive education programs. In particular, I thank my friends in executive education at UCLA's Anderson Graduate School of Management. UCLA executive education has been behind me for sixteen years and has been the most powerful of forces in helping me get my message to corporate America. From Victor Tabbush to Debra Terrill, with Alan Barnes in between and with Jim Aggen, Grace Siao, and Myra Brown as consistent supporters, the program launched me into the field of executive education. Furthermore, let's not forget that the sweet Bruins have won more NCAA basketball championships than any other top ten business school.

I also have to give my deepest gratitude to the executive education program at the University of Washington, one of the first such programs in the country to recognize the importance of building into their offerings an "emotional intelligence program." In particular, I thank Howard Norman, who, besides being a good friend, has become my valuable mentor in the executive education field.

Other schools have also provided me with the opportunity to spread my message, and teaching at the best of the best has been a most valuable learning experience. Cornell, Wharton, NYU, RPI, Tulane, University of Alabama, Penn State, Smith—have all been extremely helpful, and I certainly appreciate their belief in my work.

The Institute of Management Studies is another organization that has been very supportive of my work. Gordon Peters, Jon Peters, the IMS staff, and many of the regional chairpersons have become favorite people to work with; I am genuinely flattered that IMS praises my work.

Sue Gold has proved to be invaluable administrative assistant. I'm sure working for me is more challenging than running any marathon. She is always able to go the extra mile!

Next in line is Eric Koch who, like the rookie Jeter in '96, proved to be there in the clutch. He is very reliable, although he does not have stuff like Elliot Macht, who redeemed his poor beginning but, like Rivera, proved to be an excellent closer when the going was tough.

My two nephews give me great pleasure and are always a source of amusement. After great deliberation, I felt I had no other choice than to strip Derek, formerly known as "Sweet Meiser," of his title "Sweet" when he showed poor judgment by prematurely gloating after the Braves won the first two games and were leading 6–0 in the fourth game. The title was given instead to nephew Randy, who showed that he has the stuff of champions. "Sweet Randy": do your job!

My mother is always a great source of encouragement and optimism. She is the only person I know who can watch me on video twelve hours a day, with going to the bathroom the only interruption. She is only twenty phone rings away.

Ronnie and Don continue to be encouraging sources of motivation.

My wife, Lorie, continues to stand by my side, providing patience, understanding, support, and love.

Next, I thank the heads of the five families. My trusted friend Lee Sachs served as an encouraging soul throughout the ordeal of making a book. Morning conversations with Lee always started me out in a good mood. Steve Gold proves true to his name. Whenever I needed a favor, he was there to put me in high spirits.

Now, the three dons on the Coast. Ken Cinnamon continually proves to be the most creative consigliere of all, always supplying me with cutting-edge ideas and taking great time to help me plan out my work. He is also my only friend who is smart enough to have a Boxster! Lenny Levine is a great friend from the old days when we were like the Roman Empire. From now on, Lenny will only provide protection for my family in the West and handle only West Coast activities. You're out, Lenny—no reflection on you, but there are things that are going to happen that you must have no part in. Finally, there is Ron Podell, who always provides me with great security and great friendship. Most important, Ron has always had a knack to see the big picture—especially in his home.

I also want to thank all the other people who have shown an interest in my work and have helped me in various ways. Thank you all, and be sure to apply your emotional intelligence.

H. W.

Introduction

Nearly twenty years ago, I witnessed an exchange between two people that sparked my interest in the area of emotional intelligence. At the time, I was a graduate student working at a mental health center. One day, I was talking with a group of fellow students when a staff psychiatrist stormed in and began yelling at a woman among the group, who was studying to be a social worker. "You don't know what you're doing," he shouted, his eyes glaring. "You're causing irreparable harm to the patient!"

He went on relentlessly attacking my friend, repeating his accusations for several minutes. I felt embarrassed for her, as did the others. I was also getting angry at the psychiatrist, especially when my friend fled in tears. Even then the psychiatrist continued his barrage, telling us, "This is just typical of her defensive behavior."

The experience underscored for me that criticism, when delivered destructively, causes emotional fallout. The realization led me to look at how criticism could be used constructively, so that both the person giving it and the person receiving it gain something useful from the experience. Though I didn't know it at the time, making criticism constructive is a key element of emotional intelligence.

So is managing anger, a skill I explored two years later during my internship at a veterans hospital. While there, I noticed how many on the staff undermined their efforts by not being able to understand and defuse their anger. I noted the same problem among the patients. This led me to look at ways that people could learn to manage their anger.

Over the next few years, I saw in my own clinical studies, and learned through reading a rapidly growing body of research, that most individuals have difficulty in managing situations that are emotionally volatile, particularly when the emotions aroused are anger and anxiety. When this difficulty is coupled with poor communication skills, as was demonstrated by the psychiatrist, for example, the results can be quite disastrous.

In the 1980s, I began doing consulting work for corporations. I saw how the inability to manage emotions and communicate effectively often led to unresolved and repetitive conflicts among staff, low morale, and diminished productivity. So I began to look at how people could learn to use their emotions productively and develop the skills necessary for relating well to others.

I have continued that exploration in writing four books, carrying on a clinical and consulting practice, and giving seminars. *Emotional Intelligence at Work* represents the culmination of my work on how emotional intelligence can be used in a wide variety of companies, from Fortune 500 corporations to small businesses, from those producing widgets to those creating intellectual property, from businesses based in Manhattan to those in Miami or Milwaukee. I've learned a lot, and I'm pleased to be able to share my knowledge with you.

Definition of Emotional Intelligence

Quite simply, emotional intelligence is the intelligent use of emotions: you *intentionally* make your emotions work for you by using them to help guide your behavior and thinking in ways that enhance your results.

Let's say you have an important presentation to give and your self-awareness (a component of emotional intelligence) has pointed out to you that you're feeling extremely anxious. Your emotional intelligence then leads you to undertake a number of actions: you might take charge of any destructive thoughts; use relaxation to diminish your arousal; and cease any counterproductive behaviors, such as pacing about the room. In so doing, you reduce your anxiety sufficiently so that you can confidently make your presentation.

Applications of emotional intelligence in the workplace are almost infinite. Emotional intelligence is instrumental in resolving a sticky problem with a coworker, closing a deal with a difficult customer, criticizing your boss, staying on top of a task until it is completed, and in many other challenges affecting your success. Emotional intelligence is used both intrapersonally (helping yourself) and interpersonally (helping others).

The Building Blocks of Emotional Intelligence

Your emotional intelligence derives from four basic elements that operate like the building blocks of DNA. If nurtured with experience, these elements enable you to develop specific skills and abilities, the basis of your emotional intelligence. Unlike your biological DNA, however, your emotional intelligence building blocks can be developed so that you can dramatically increase your emotional intelligence. These four building blocks were identified by the pioneering psychologists John Mayer of the University of New Hampshire and Peter Salovey of Yale, who also coined the term *emotional intelligence* in 1990.

Each building block represents abilities that together give rise to your emotional intelligence. They are hierarchical, with each level incorporating and building upon the capabilities of all previous ones. The four building blocks are:

1. The ability to accurately perceive, appraise, and express emotion

2. The ability to access or generate feelings on demand when they can facilitate understanding of yourself or another person

3. The ability to understand emotions and the knowledge that derives from them

4. The ability to regulate emotions to promote emotional and intellectual growth

Throughout the book, we see how each of these building blocks helps develop the particular skills that together form our emotional intelligence.

Emotional Intelligence at Work

In the last four years, much research has been conducted in the field of emotional intelligence. Studies have covered such areas as identifying methods for measuring emotional intelligence, determining the importance of emotional intelligence skills to one's effectiveness, and applying and integrating emotional intelligence in a variety of settings, including schoolrooms.

In this book, I have chosen to focus specifically on the application of emotional intelligence in the workplace because that's where I've seen a critical need. During nearly twenty years' working as a consulting psychologist to dozens of companies and public agencies, I have seen how the lack of emotional intelligence undermines both an individual's and a company's growth and success, and conversely how the use of emotional intelligence leads to productive outcomes at both the individual and the organizational levels. I've also seen that when employees use their emotional intelligence, they help build an emotionally intelligent organization, one in which everyone takes responsibility for increasing their own emotional intelligence, for using it in their relations with others, and for applying the skills of emotional intelligence to the organization as a whole.

Through conducting my seminars, I've discovered that employees want to learn very specifically how they can apply the skills of emotional intelligence to their own work situations. They are not concerned with the theoretical but with the very practical aspects of emotional intelligence. So I've written *Emotional Intelligence at Work* to be easy to follow and hands-on, the goal being for you to tap into, develop, and use your emotional intelligence as easily, efficiently, and effectively as possible.

To this end, I have included scores of examples that illustrate real-world applications of emotional intelligence far better than any pedagogical discussion might. I've also included dozens of exercises that offer a clear, step-by-step approach to learning a particular technique, for example, tuning into changes in your arousal level. And you will find many tips suggesting precise ways you can use a skill most productively.

Throughout the book, you also come across sections headed "Emotional Intelligence at Work." These are first-person accounts I've collected over the years from individuals who participated in my seminars at Fortune 500 companies, federal government agencies, the army, hospitals, school systems, and business schools. (I've used pseudonyms and changed identifying details to ensure anonymity.) I hope these accounts help you see even more clearly what I reinforce throughout the book: that emotional intelligence *does* work.

Emotional Intelligence at Work is divided into two parts. The first concerns the *intrapersonal* use of your emotional intelligence: how to develop and use it with regard to yourself. The second part deals with *interpersonal* use: how to be more effective in your relationships with others.

Part One: Increasing Your Emotional Intelligence

Chapter One: Developing High Self-Awareness

With high self-awareness you are able to monitor yourself, observe yourself in action, to influence your actions so that they work to your benefit. By being aware, for example, that your voice is getting louder and you are becoming increasingly angry at a client who is making yet another unreasonable demand—and recognizing, of

course, how important your client is to your ongoing employment—
you might lower your voice, defuse your anger, and respond to your
client respectfully. We begin Chapter One by looking at how high
self-awareness is the foundation upon which all other emotional
intelligence skills are built. Then we explore how you can develop
high self-awareness: by tuning into the wealth of information—your
interpretations, thoughts, feelings, senses, emotions, and intentions—
available to you about yourself.

Chapter Two: Managing Your Emotions

Unlike suppressing your emotions, which deprives you of the valuable information your emotions can give you, managing your emotions means understanding them and then using that understanding
to deal with situations productively. Because emotions are produced
by an interaction of your thoughts, physiological changes, and
behavioral actions in response to an external event, you can manage your emotions by taking charge of each component, as we see
in Chapter Two. Then, because a distressful emotion is generally
caused by a problem situation—you're feeling fearful because of
the impending restructuring of your department—we look next at
how you can bring your emotional thermostat to a level that
allows you to think productively. You can then use problem solving to come up with the best course of action to take to resolve
the situation.

Chapter Three: Motivating Yourself

When you are self-motivated, you are able to begin a task or assignment, stick with it, and move ahead to completion, all the while
dealing with any setbacks that may arise. Fortunately, there are
resources you can draw upon for motivation, and we look at them
in this chapter: yourself; supportive friends, family, and colleagues;
an emotional mentor (an inspirational figure, real or fictitious); and
your environment (the air, lights, sounds in your office). These
sources help you become and remain motivated through encourag-

ing and bolstering your confidence, optimism, tenacity, enthusiasm, and resiliency, and by helping you turn setbacks—from a recalcitrant report to job termination—into comebacks.

Part Two: Using Your Emotional Intelligence in Your Relations with Others

Chapter Four: Developing Effective Communication Skills

The basis of any relationship is communication. Communication establishes connection, and connection forges a relationship. The value of effective communication skills in the workplace is incalculable. Think of trying to resolve a conflict with a coworker, or speaking to your boss about her insensitivity, or listening to a client's complaints without being able to communicate well. Wrong words, ill-advised gestures, or misunderstood meanings can lead to very unsatisfactory outcomes. In Chapter Four, you learn five skills that can ensure that your exchanges with others have the greatest chance for positive outcomes: self-disclosure, assertiveness, dynamic listening, criticism, and team communication.

Chapter Five: Developing Interpersonal Expertise

Relating well to others means connecting with them to exchange information meaningfully and appropriately. If you consider how much of your day is devoted to dealing with others, you can readily understand why "relates well to others" is so often listed as a desired qualification in job descriptions. What enables you to relate well to others is interpersonal expertise. In this chapter, we look at what constitutes a relationship (meeting each others' needs; relating to each other over time; and sharing feelings, thoughts, and ideas). Then we explore the two skills that lead to interpersonal expertise: the ability to analyze a relationship so that you can navigate a productive course through it, and the ability to communicate at appropriate levels so that information is exchanged effectively.

Chapter Six: Helping Others Help Themselves

A work organization is an integrated system that depends upon the interrelationship of the individuals who are part of it. That's why it's so important to the success of a company not only that all employees perform to the best of their abilities but also that they help others do the same. In the context of emotional intelligence, this means helping others to manage their emotions, communicate effectively, solve their problems, resolve their conflicts, and become motivated. In the final chapter, we look at four specific ways you can do just that: by keeping your emotional perspective, knowing how to calm an out-of-control person, being a supportive listener, and helping with goal planning and goal reaching. Finally, in Chapter Six we see how your ability to help others, together with your interpersonal expertise and your own emotional intelligence, can help create an emotionally intelligent organization.

My Three Wishes

I include a great deal of information in this book about how you can productively use your emotional intelligence in the workplace. Some information you'll be able to grasp and make use of use almost immediately, while other information may take you a little longer to see as relevant and to adapt.

But beyond the practical aspects of emotional intelligence that we cover extensively, there are three points I wish you to keep in mind as you read this book and go to work each day. The first is how important emotions are in the workplace and to your own performance there. Although emotions are powerful influences on our behavior, for many years it has been considered inappropriate to show—or even to have—emotions in a work situation, as if our emotional makeup is irrelevant to business. Currently, however, an overwhelming amount of research shows that not only are emotions very much a part of the work experience but, to a large degree, they set the course that a company follows. This book shows you dozens of examples of how this is so.

My second wish is that you fully grasp the impact that developing your emotional intelligence can have on your success in the workplace. Because most of us are presumably driven by the desire for success, whether job satisfaction or higher promotions, once we understand how our emotional intelligence can lead to professional success, we will be motivated to use the skills of emotional intelligence to our best abilities.

My final wish is that you comprehend the need to help others develop their own emotional intelligence with a view to building an emotionally intelligent organization. You need only imagine what it might be like to work in a company where, for example, everyone communicates with understanding and respect, where people set group goals and help others work toward them, and where enthusiasm and confidence in the organization are widespread, to be sufficiently inspired to encourage the development of emotional intelligence among all the employees in your company.

These were my goals in writing this book. I hope that my emotional intelligence was operating at a sufficiently high level that they can be accomplished.

August 1997   HENDRIE WEISINGER, PH.D.
Westport, Connecticut

To Briana and Daniel,
my true treasures

Emotional Intelligence at Work

Part One

Increasing Your Emotional Intelligence

Your emotions can give you valuable information—about yourself, other people, and situations. An angry outburst unleashed on a coworker might let you know that you are feeling overwhelmed by an unreasonable workload. Anxiety about an upcoming presentation could tell you that you need to be better prepared with facts and figures. Frustration with a client might suggest you need to find other ways of getting her to respond to you. By tapping in to the information that your emotions provide, you are able to alter your behavior and thinking in such a way that you can turn situations around. In the case of the angry outburst, for example, you might see the importance of taking action to reduce your workload or streamline your work process.

Emotions, as you can see, play an important role in the workplace. From anger to elation, frustration to contentment, you confront emotions—yours and others'—on a daily basis at the office. The key is to use your emotions intelligently, which is just what we mean by emotional intelligence: you intentionally make your emotions work for you by using them to help guide your behavior and thinking in ways that enhance your results.

The good news is that emotional intelligence can be nurtured, developed, and augmented—it isn't a trait that you either have or don't have. You increase your emotional intelligence by learning and practicing the skills and capabilities that make up emotional intelligence. These include self-awareness, emotional management, and self-motivation.

In Part One, we look at how you can increase your emotional intelligence through developing high self-awareness, learning how to manage your emotions, and becoming adept at motivating yourself. Once you are familiar with how to use your emotional intelligence with regard to yourself, we move on to Part Two and see how you can use your emotional intelligence to ensure that your relations with clients, coworkers, managers, customers, and colleagues are as productive as possible.

Developing High Self-Awareness

During the course of a workday, you might speak with an angry client, respond to an anxious boss's concerns, present an idea in a meeting. How you perform each of these activities is influenced by a number of factors. For example, if the angry client has been making one unreasonable demand after another, then you might very well be short-tempered with him. If you're confident about your role in a project, then you will probably be able to allay your boss's concerns. If you believe your coworkers suspect you are too inexperienced for your job, you might feel shy and insecure in presenting your ideas to them in a meeting.

Being aware of your feelings and behavior as well as others' perceptions of you can influence your actions in such a way that they work to your benefit. Let's say, in the first example, you are aware that your client is driving you crazy, and you also know that alienating him could have unfortunate consequences. Your course of action might be to mollify him rather than to further anger him with your short temper. In the second case, that of the anxious boss, if you sense how distressed she is because such a lot depends on the success of this particular project, then you might take extra care in telling her what you've done and reassuring her that the project will be well received. In the last example, if you are aware that your coworkers perceive you as being inexperienced, then you'll probably want to be fully prepared before presenting your idea.

The key here is tuning into the wealth of information—your feelings, senses, appraisals, actions, and intentions—available to you about yourself. This information helps you understand how you respond, behave, communicate, and operate in different situations. Processing this information is what we mean by self-awareness. In this chapter, we look at how developing high self-awareness can help you be more effective in the workplace.

Why High Self-Awareness Is the Basic Building Block of Emotional Intelligence

As we learned in the Introduction, you can enhance your emotional intelligence by learning how to manage your emotions and motivate yourself. You can maximize the effectiveness of your emotional intelligence by developing good communication skills, interpersonal expertise, and mentoring abilities. Self-awareness is the core of each of these skills, because emotional intelligence can only begin when affective information enters the perceptual system. As examples, to be able to manage your anger you must be aware of what triggers it and how this powerful emotion first comes upon you; then you can learn to diminish it and use it appropriately. To short-circuit dejection so that you can motivate yourself, you must be aware of how you allow negative statements about yourself to sabotage your work. To help others help themselves, you must be aware of your emotional involvement in the relationship.

High self-awareness enables you to monitor yourself, to observe yourself in action. Given that you are at the center of your universe, you must first understand what it is that makes you do what you do before you can begin to alter your actions for better results. You must understand what is important to you, how you experience things, what you want, how you feel, and how you come across to others. This subjective knowledge about the nature of your personality not only guides your behavior from situation to situation, as we see in these simple examples; it also provides you with a solid framework for making better choices. These can be minor matters (*Which cold call should I make first?*) or major choices (*If I take that new job, I'll be in a workgroup with fifty people, and I know those kinds of situations make me feel threatened and shy. If I stay here, I'll make less money, but I'll feel comfortable and safe, and this is what I need right now.*).

To effectively navigate through your work world, to know what course you are to follow and how to stay on it, you need a gyroscope. Think of your self-awareness that way: it helps keep you centered and immediately alerts you when you are tilting off course.

How Low Self-Awareness Can Handicap Your Actions

In one of my seminars a few years ago, a screenwriter—we'll call him Larry—told of an unfortunate encounter he once had with a network producer. He had submitted his recent screenplay, on which he had worked extraordinarily hard, to the producer. When they met to discuss it, the producer told him that this was one of the worst scripts she had ever read. "She was harsh and angry," Larry said. A few days later, Larry ran into the producer in the studio commissary. He decided to tell her how distressed he had been by her treatment of him. "She was astonished," he said. "She denied that she was either harsh or angry, and she wasn't being defensive—she really believed that."

Clearly, the producer lacked awareness of how she came across to Larry, and also of what her real feelings were (anger that the script was not what she had wanted, frustration that her time was being wasted). Not only did she alienate Larry, who said he would never again submit a script to her, but she eventually lost her job.

In the three opening examples, we easily see how low self-awareness can lead to very different outcomes. Not recognizing your anger at your client and thus being unable to manage it, you might shout and yell at him, thereby derailing your relationship with the client. By not understanding the distress your boss is feeling, you might dismiss her concerns, causing her more distress and a lack of confidence in your abilities. And by not perceiving your coworkers' doubts about your abilities, you may not prepare well for the meeting, thereby giving them ample justification for their doubts.

Lacking self-awareness, you lack sufficient information to make effective decisions. Presumably you wouldn't decide to go with one vendor over another without getting adequate background information about each of the candidates, because by doing so you handicap your decision. Similarly, when you operate from a position of low self-awareness, you handicap your response to people and situations by approaching them with inadequate information.

How to Increase Your Self-Awareness

We've suggested that self-awareness is the key to emotional intelligence, that it's important to your success in the workplace, and that not having it can handicap your effectiveness. Now we examine how you can increase your self-awareness. Be assured that hours of expensive psychotherapy are not required here. What you need to increase your self-awareness is some serious thoughtfulness and the courage to explore how you react to the people and events in your worklife. Specifically, you have to (1) examine how you make appraisals, (2) tune in to your senses, (3) get in touch with your feelings, (4) learn what your intentions are, and (5) pay attention to your actions.

Examine How You Make Appraisals

Appraisals are all the different impressions, interpretations, evaluations, and expectations you have about yourself, other people, and situations. They are influenced by the various factors that shape your personality (family background, previous experiences, natural abilities, systems of belief), and they generally take the form of thoughts or an inner dialogue (*This presentation is going to be a dis-*

aster. I'm going to blow this deal.). By becoming aware of your appraisals, you learn how your thoughts influence your feelings, actions, and reactions, and you can thus alter them accordingly.

In the case of the presentation, for example, the impression you have of yourself is that you can't handle the situation. The expectation you have of the outcome is that it will be a complete failure. This negative appraisal can lead to a self-fulfilling prophecy (because of your fears about the presentation, you will be perceptively nervous, appear not to be in control of the facts or the situation, and indeed blow the deal). But if you recognize that you tend to put a negative spin on your appraisals, you can try to give a positive spin to your inner dialogue (*I'm going to do fine; I have all the facts at hand, the points are all in order*). This enables you to reassure yourself, relax, and make the presentation clearly and effectively.

■■■

Tips for Becoming Aware of How You Make Appraisals

Use *I-Think* Statements.

These are statements that begin with "I think": "I think that's a good idea." "I think we should meet with those people." "I think he is not working as hard as he could be." By intentionally using *I-think* statements, you help clarify what you think, and you also recognize that you are the person responsible for your appraisals (this is important, as we shall see below).

Regularly Engage in an Inner Dialogue.

This is the talk that you have with yourself, as in the case of the person before the presentation. You pick a regular time during the day and talk with yourself. "I think my boss was being unreasonable when she asked me to process more orders than I had ever done before." "I'm still having a hard time working with Clara." "I think the presentation went very well." Gradually, you become aware of any patterns to your inner dialogue; perhaps they always reflect an insecurity, often raise doubts, or always seem to take the positive route. By seeing patterns, you can then examine whether or not your inner dialogue works for or against you. For example, raising doubts (*I think the new schedule is not going to work out*) can often be a good thing because it causes you to question policies, decisions, and actions. On the other hand, if you always have doubts, you might be resistant to change, which is likely to work against you.

Reflect on Encounters When You Are Calm.

Take a few minutes after a meeting with your boss, a coworker, or the whole staff to ask yourself what influenced your appraisal of the encounter. Let's say you met with your boss and came out of the meeting saying to yourself, "She doesn't know what she's talking about." You might ask yourself if this is really the case. Or is it that she just doesn't agree with you but really *does* know what she's talking about? You might also clarify whether the fact that your boss was promoted to that position, which you were also being considered for, causes you to see everything that she says as being wrong. By having this inner dialogue when you are calm, your appraisals are likely to be more flexible and rational; this helps you draw accurate conclusions. If you appraise encounters when you are agitated, your conclusions are more likely to be inaccurate.

Seek Input from Others.

Because any event can be appraised from different perspectives, it's often a good idea to ask others for their appraisal of the event. In the example with the boss, if others were also there you might ask them if they felt your boss was on the right track, if she was in control of the facts, if she presented them logically. Their responses might help you see if your appraisal of the encounter was way off base, spot on, or somewhere in between.

■■■

By becoming aware of how you make appraisals, you increase your chances of making fair, accurate, and perceptive ones. But because they are so subjective, there is the chance that you can carry them too far, ignoring other people's appraisals or assuming that yours are fixed. There is also the chance that you don't take your appraisals far enough: you don't recognize their effect on your reaction, and you don't trust their accuracy.

Here are some points to keep in mind as you learn how you make appraisals.

■■■

Tips for Making Accurate Appraisals

Remember That Appraisal, Not Behavior, Causes Reaction.

Recognize that it is your appraisals, not someone else's behavior or an event, that cause your reactions. It is the meaning we assign to events and to people we encounter that affects us for good or ill, not the events or people themselves. Let's say you make a presentation about how your office can be more ergonomically sound. When you finish, everyone says what great suggestions you have, how thoroughly you looked into the topic. Afterward you may think to yourself, "They made my day." *They* didn't. What makes you feel elated is that you appraise your presentation as having been a great success. Conversely, if you feel disappointed after listening to negative comments about your presentation, your disappointment would be due to your appraisal, not to your coworkers' criticism. By making this distinction, you empower yourself with your own success or failure. This is important, because we don't want others to have that power over us.

Acknowledge Your Appraisals Are Your Own.

Take note of your appraisals while making room for those of others. As was suggested, different people may interpret the same event differently. Although your appraisal is valid for you, theirs are valid for them, and you need to respect that. Suppose you and a colleague are interviewing a person for a receptionist's position. After the interview, you say that you think Michael, the interviewee, doesn't really want the job because he didn't ask any questions. Your colleague says that she thinks Michael does want the job; she thinks he looked enthusiastic and assumes that as he was a receptionist elsewhere for so long, he didn't want to waste your time by asking questions he knew he could answer once he started working. Your appraisal is valid for you, and your colleague's is for her.

Accept That Appraisals Are Subject to Change.

It is important to recognize that your thoughts, feelings, and appraisals are not immutable; they are subject to change based on new information to which your self-awareness antennae alert you. Let's say after your interview with Michael, the receptionist candidate, you pass by the reception area of your office and see him and the current receptionist talking. You overhear that Michael is finding out from her more about the job. This new information probably causes you to revise your appraisal of Michael as not being interested in the job. This doesn't mean that your earlier appraisal wasn't accurate at the time; it was, given your perceptions of the situation and the information you had then.

■■■

Tune in to Your Senses

Your senses—seeing, hearing, smelling, tasting, and touching—are the sources of all your data about the world. It is through your senses that you pick up information about yourself, other people, and different situations. But a funny thing often happens to our senses: they are filtered and transformed by our appraisals. Let's go back to the example of your boss, whom you think is a jerk and not up to the job. During the meeting she said that she had not had a chance to look more into the question under discussion, as she had been busy with other things, but she wanted the meeting to be a preliminary discussion of the issues. You were so convinced of her incompetence that you didn't hear her say this. You therefore dismissed her inadequate grasp of the subject as being due to stupidity rather than insufficient time. Your appraisal of her performance then acted as a filter, obliterating some important things she was saying. The higher your self-awareness, the greater your ability to take the filtering process into account and make the distinction between sensory data and appraisals.

Distinguish Between Sensory Data and Appraisals

In my seminars, I often have the participants do an exercise that clearly points out this distinction. I ask them to have a three-minute conversation with a partner and then report the sense data they observe in each other. I tell them to ignore appraisals, feelings, and conclusions. Still, that's hard to do, as these typical responses suggest:

> "You look sad."
>
> "I see that you're making nervous movements with your foot."
>
> "I think you're enthusiastic."

Sad, nervous, and enthusiastic are all appraisals. Now, here's what the relevant sense data might be:

> "I see a frown, a sagging chin."
>
> "I feel the vibrations from your shaking foot."
>
> "I hear you talking quickly, with a lilt in your voice."

It's easy to see from this list how sense data can be misinterpreted. In the case of the person with the frown and sagging chin, she could simply be concentrating, rather than sad. To interpret that data as indicating sadness, we need more information (say, her manager has said that he often sees her sitting by herself in the lunchroom, staring off into space, and has overheard angry phone conversations with her husband).

Sense data can sometimes seem contradictory. The person described as enthusiastic might be observed pacing back and forth in her office, sitting at the computer for a while but writing nothing, taking long cigarette breaks. These data do not suggest enthusiasm, but instead procrastination. On the other hand, the pacing and apparent avoidance might actually be this person's unique way of getting into a project; indeed, the next day she might be seen sitting typing away for hours, seemingly enthusiastic about the project.

By being able to tune into your senses, you can check, clarify, and alter your appraisals when needed. Here are some exercises to help you increase your sensory awareness.

■■■

Exercises to Help You Tune in to Your Senses

While Walking Down the Street

1. Take deep breaths and try to identify as many different smells as you can: the wet-metal smell from the subway grate, the sweet-soap smell of dryer steam in the breeze.

2. Pay close attention to all the sounds you can hear, particularly those you usually tune out: a car door closing a block away, a plane in the distance, a baby crying inside an apartment.

3. Focus on everything your body is feeling: your sleeves against your arm (soft? scratchy?), your foot in your shoe (cramped? springy?), the surface under foot (hard? uneven?).

You can adapt this exercise to sitting at your desk, at the dinner table, or anywhere. The value of it is to sharpen your awareness of your senses, which facilitates differentiating between sensory data and appraisals. This helps you in relying upon the information your senses give you to make accurate appraisals (*it was an unpleasant walk because of the subway smells, my scratchy pants, the uneven road surface*).

During a Meeting

At the next office meeting, try to gauge the mood of the group by relying only on sensory data. Presumably your senses of taste, touch, and smell will not be providing data here, so use seeing and hearing.

1. Seeing. Pay attention to how people look at one another while they are speaking and listening. Do they look straight in the eye? (This might indicate confidence.) Does the speaker look at everyone or just focus on one individual? (The former could reflect comfort with the group as a whole, and a sense of the group being a team.) Do the listeners stay focused on the speaker, or do their eyes wander? (The former suggests interest in what the person is saying, the latter disinterest.) Do you see people smile, frown, glare, smirk?

2. Hearing. Tune in to the sounds in the room, people's voices. When a person talks, is there quiet except for that person's voice, or do you hear people moving in their chairs? (The former suggests interest in what the speaker is saying, the latter perhaps boredom.) Do people speak stridently? (This might reflect anger, frustration.) Haltingly? (This might reflect lack of knowledge of the subject.) Do you hear a lot of mumbled conversations while someone is talking? (This could suggest enthusiasm, if they like what the person has to say but have more to comment; or disapproval, as they express their disagreement to their neighbors.) Do people yell, whisper, whine, interrupt?

3. At the end of the meeting, look at all the raw data you've collected and see what you can deduce about the mood of the group, based solely on that data. (The staff were enthusiastic about the proposed ergonomic changes to the office; they seemed pleased that management was willing to do this; they appeared to want to work together as a group to implement the changes; they all seemed to grasp the importance of making the changes.)

This exercise clearly shows how sensory data influence your appraisals. Being aware of how this happens enables you to rely more on your senses and therefore derive more accurate appraisals from them.

■■■

Get in Touch with Your Feelings

Your feelings are your spontaneous emotional responses to the inter-pretations you make and the expectations you have. Like sensory data, they provide important information that helps you understand why you do what you do. They alert you to your comfort level in a situation, and they help you understand your reactions. That's why tuning in to your feelings is so important.

Let's say you've had a difficult day at work. Your boss dumped a new project on you, when you already have more than you can manage, and the information you needed for a report due tomorrow hasn't arrived. When you get home your daughter rushes to greet you at the door, jumping up and down, trying to show you a picture she made. You yell at her and tell her to go to her room. Outwardly it seems as though you are angry at your daughter. But if you stop to ask yourself what is really going on, you realize that you're feeling very angry with your boss and frustrated with the amount of work you have to do. Your daughter did the same thing she does every day, something that usually causes you to pick her up, hug her, and sit and look at her drawings. If instead, as you drive home, you try to tune in to the uneasiness you are feeling and identify it as anger and frus-tration, you might avoid the misplaced outburst at your daughter.

Tuning into our emotions is not something that comes easily to most of us. Part of the problem is that to tune into feelings—especially distressful ones such as anger, sadness, and resentment—we need to experience them, and that can be painful. So we ignore them, deny them, or rationalize them. By doing this, we may enable ourselves not to feel bad at the moment, but at the same time we are prevented from making use of the valuable information these feelings could give us and thus cannot use our emotions intelligently.

Let's say you're furious with Emily, your coworker because she's just not doing her share of work and you're picking up her slack. You don't discuss your anger with anyone. You pretend you're not angry, but just overworked. You tell yourself that Emily is young and therefore doesn't understand fully what she should be doing. You are sharp-tongued with her, and tired and irritable at home, for no reason you can ascertain. But if instead you tune in to your anger and resentment by asking yourself what's really going on here, you can see that it's your perception of Emily's inability to do the job that is making you angry. By acknowledging the anger, you then give yourself the opportunity to manage it productively. You might go out to lunch with Emily and ask her if she's having trouble with the job, if there's some way you can help her. You might speak to your boss about the problem.

We deal more with managing your emotions in the next chapter. The point here is that by ignoring or denying your emotions you deny yourself the ability to work through them. Negative feelings can often fester, leaving you feeling worse than you would by tuning in to them. By acknowledging them, you are able to manage them and move on.

Although it's difficult to get in touch with your feelings, it is by no means impossible. Like all the other steps in developing high self-awareness, this requires learning and practice. The following tips facilitate awareness of your feelings.

■■■

Tips for Getting in Touch with Your Feelings

Become Attuned to the Corresponding Physical Manifestations.

Although feelings are internal, they often have outward manifestations. By paying attention to these outward signs, you can begin to understand the feelings they reflect. For example, if you find your face getting warm during a conversation, you might be embarrassed. If you feel your stomach astir, you may be nervous. If you feel your body relaxed in the chair, you might be quite at ease with the person. In this last case, let's say the person you are talking with is a potential employer. After the job interview, you wonder how you would feel working with that person. She seems very exacting in what she wants you to do, and she makes you question whether or not you actually have the requisite skills. On the other hand, you felt very comfortable and relaxed in the chair, so perhaps she is someone you would feel at ease working with.

Become Attuned to the Corresponding Behavioral Manifestations.
Feelings often drive certain behaviors. By working backwards again, that is, by examining the behavioral manifestation, we can often learn what the feeling is. For example, if you find yourself clenching the arm of your chair with your hand while having a conversation, you may be angry. If you're tapping your pencil on the desk, you might be anxious. If you notice that you're smiling, you are probably happy. These behavioral signs are all clues to what your feelings are.

■■■

The following is an exercise that will help you get in touch with your feelings.

■■■

Exercise: Keep a Feeling Journal

In case this sounds like a grade-school exercise to you, consider that first-year MBA students at Northwestern University's preeminent business school are required to keep a Feeling Journal during their first year. The reason why, and the reason I recommend this exercise to you, is that first of all this is an excellent way to become more aware of your emotions in general. Secondly, it enables you to become aware of the role your emotions play in your work life.

Here's what you do:

1. At different times during the day, or at the end of each workday, jot down in a little notebook what feelings you experienced during the preceding hours, and what caused them. This might be relief that the transport company got back to you, anxiety that the work order wouldn't go out in time, joy that your vacation days were approved, or fear because five people were laid off. Write all of them down, regardless of how insubstantial they might seem.

2. At the end of a few weeks, or a month, look back over your entries. Do you find you have certain emotions more often than others (for example, are you angry a lot of the time)? Do you have the same feelings over and over, from the same cause (constant anxiety because of delays in work orders)? In this examination of your feelings, you can see if there might be some changes you could make, say, to alleviate anxiety. If not, as in the case of fear of being laid off, then you might try to figure out how to work through that emotion so it doesn't interfere with your workday. (We go over this in the next chapter, on managing your emotions.)

■■■

The Feeling Journal enables you to see what emotions you experience and which ones recur. You can use this knowledge to explore why you are having certain emotions and, if they are negative ones, how you can alter the situation to avoid having them. Through looking over your journal, you can also get a sense of which emotions you are *not* experiencing. Let's say you're not feeling contentment or joy. You may ask yourself why that is so, and see what you can do about it.

■■■

Exercise: Mentally Revisit a Distressful Situation

I'm sure this exercise sounds like a lot of fun. . . . But it has enormous value, because by reexperiencing in your mind a difficult or painful experience, you learn more about how you react emotionally to situations and you cause the emotion to seem less formidable.

We are often reluctant to get in touch with distressful emotions, yet those are usually the ones from which we can learn the most. It is useful to understand how we can tap into those emotions. Here's an exercise for learning to do that.

1. Bring into focus the distressful situation. To do this, pick a quiet time and space. Close your eyes. Call up in your mind the experience that caused you to feel depressed, sad, hurt.

2. Try to reconstruct the setting as clearly as you can. This helps you get in touch with the emotions better. Suppose your manager called you into his office, saying he wanted to talk with you. You went in and sat down. You could see the snow piled up on the warehouse rooftop. You saw the photos of his children on his desk. You could hear the trucks coming and going outside. You were sitting on an uncomfortable plastic chair.

3. Try to reconstruct the conversation. "Janine," he said, "I have to tell you that your output is considerably below the other people's in your group. You know we're in a big crunch to get product into the market before the beginning of the new year. I don't know what's going on with you, but I'd sure like you to tell me, because if you can't do the job, I've got a long list of names of people who can."

4. Try to reexperience the emotions you felt during that encounter. The shame at having your work put down and your abilities questioned. The anger at your manager's unreasonableness (your task was much more complicated than those of the other people in the group). The terror that you would lose your job and not find another, and you and your children would become homeless. The hurt that your manager didn't recognize the dedication you had shown those many years, even when benefits had been cut.

5. Ask yourself if your emotions seemed appropriate. The terror was probably an overreaction; you didn't really believe your boss would fire you. The shame was offbase, too; you were actually quite convinced that you worked as hard as anyone could have, given the circumstances.

At the end of this exercise, you should gain certain insights. For example, you discover that you tend to exaggerate the negative consequences of a situation (that you will be fired), and you readily feel shame even when it's not warranted. Presumably, these realizations help reduce the impact of the emotions and allow you to have some relief.

■■■

Learn What Your Intentions Are

Intentions can refer to your immediate desires: what you would like to accomplish today, in a specific situation, in the coming week. They can also refer to long-term desires: what you would like to have done at the end of the year, or over the course of your lifetime. For the purposes of this book, we refer just to the short-term intentions, as I find these are the ones with which people often have more difficulty.

The value in becoming fully aware of your intentions is that you can use the information to help better strategize your course of action. Suppose you'd like to know what it is you really want from your client. Do you want her to:

1. Agree to a sale as quickly as possible?
2. Keep you on as her primary supplier?
3. Be impressed with you so she'll recommend others to you?

If you decide that:

1. What you really want is the quick sale, then you might drop your price
2. What you want is a long-term supplier relationship, then you might drop the price and expend a great deal of energy in satisfying her every wish
3. You want to impress her, then you need to work as hard as you can for her

Like feelings, your intentions can sometimes be difficult to discern. In the case of feelings, the reason is that we often deny them or ignore them, because they are uncomfortable to face. But with intentions, the reason is that we often confuse one intention with another: we see our apparent intention but not our hidden agenda.

As an example, your intention may appear to be that you want to get promoted to a vice presidency. But your hidden agenda might be that you want your parents, who always thought you wouldn't amount to anything, to be impressed with your success. In this case, recognizing that your true intention is to impress your parents does not necessarily mean altering your plan to pursue the vice presidency; the recognition simply clarifies that this is the *true* intention.

Another difficulty with intentions is that they sometimes seem to conflict with one another. For example, you want to yell at your secretary because you're furious that she forgot to give you an important message. But you also want her to feel comfortable working with you, which she wouldn't if you were to yell at her. If you ascertain that your true intention is to have a good working relationship with your secretary, then you are more likely to manage your anger and less likely to yell when she errs.

The following are some ideas to help you clarify your intentions.

■■■

Tips for Learning What Your Intentions Are

Believe Your Behavior.

Generally, when you do something you do it because you want to do it, or at least because you feel there is something to be gained from doing it. In this way, your behavior is a good clue to your intentions. Suppose, much to your dismay, you tell your boss you'll work on Christmas day. What are you thinking? Your family will be furious, you're already burned out, and you need the day off. The decision is a clue to what your intention is: to have your boss think of you as hard-working and amenable, so that he will consider you for an upcoming promotion. By using your behavior as a clue, you can better understand what your real intentions are.

Trust Your Feelings.

If you feel happy, satisfied, or content when you are in a certain situation, then there's a good chance you chose that situation for a valid reason. In the case of what you want from the client above, let's say you decide that choice two is the course of action to follow: you want to develop a long-term supplier relationship with her. So you drop the price, you make sure that she gets her orders on time, and you develop an invoicing system that better meets her needs. You find that you are content doing all of this. This contentment suggests that your real intention is indeed to work at developing a long-term relationship. Conversely, if you take the same steps but begin to resent all the time it is taking you to satisfy your client's needs, then you are justified in assuming that perhaps your true intention is choice one, a quick sale.

Be Honest with Yourself.

Here's where the hidden agendas come in. In the example of wanting to impress your parents, you might have to ask yourself some pointed questions to figure out your intention. More money isn't the issue, as there is a negligible salary increase. Defeating the person who is also up for the promotion is not your intention, since your boss has already reprimanded him for having jeopardized your last project. Your brother was always held up as being the perfect child; do you want to get back at him? He isn't responsible for that childhood treatment. What you really want is to show your parents that you, too, are a capable, successful person; you believe that's what the vice presidency would indicate.

■■■

Pay Attention to Your Actions

In this chapter, we have looked at four areas of self-awareness: your appraisals, senses, feelings, and intentions. We've discussed how they can often be difficult to discern because they involve internal cognitive, sensory, and emotional processes. Now we come to the fifth area, your actions. Because actions are physical, they can be observed by others, and we can observe them if we choose to. Note that *choose* is the operative word here.

Even though we are generally aware of our broad actions (*I'm walking to the meeting; I'm sitting in a chair; I'm talking during the meeting*), we are often not aware of the nuances of those actions: *I'm walking slowly, I'm sitting slumped in my chair, I'm interrupting the speakers each time I open my mouth.* Yet it is these nuances that are frequently apparent to others. They may be considered clues to our attitudes and behavior.

Here's how others might interpret those actions. You're walking slowly to the meeting because you don't want to attend it. You're sitting slumped in your chair because you are disinterested in the discussion and don't wish to be part of it. You keep interrupting because you are rude and don't care to hear what anyone else has to say.

Now, let's suppose this is what's actually going on. You're walking slowly because you are getting your thoughts together. You sit slumped in your chair because you're tired and your back hurts. You interrupt because you have lots of ideas and are eager to have your comments heard. It's easy to see why becoming aware of all these unconscious actions—speech patterns, body language, nonverbal behavior—enables you to help others perceive you more accurately. Here are some ways you can learn to do that.

■■■

Tips for Increasing Your Awareness of Your Actions

Monitor Your Actions.

Choose an action that you might carry out in a meeting; it could be listening, talking, sitting. Focus on this action in several different meetings so you can uncover any patterns. Suppose you choose listening. Do you look the speaker in the eye while listening, or do you look away? Do you nod at some things the speaker says? at everything? at nothing? Do you fidget or doodle, or do you stay still? Let's say you choose talking. Do you interrupt, or do you wait until the other person has finished? Do you take long pauses with "uhs" in between? Do you look down as you talk? at one person? at many people?

Once you discover patterns, think about what they imply. For example, if you nod constantly while someone else is talking, the speaker might assume you agree with everything she says and that you want to hear more—which may not be the case. When you talk, if you pause and say "uh" a lot, people might think your grasp of the subject is a little weak, or that you are indecisive, or you take too long to think. By becoming aware of these actions, you are able to change them so they work better for you: speak without pausing, or nod only when you want the speaker to think you are in agreement.

Observe the Impact of Your Actions.

Choose an action. It could be smiling at people you see in the hall-way, returning phone calls, using the copy machine. Pay attention to the responses you get. Do people smile back? Do they then initiate conversation? Do they acknowledge you later in the cafeteria? Let's say you usually wait several days before returning phone calls. Do you find that people are peeved when you finally get back to them? Do they then make *you* wait several days before they get back to you? In using the copy machine, suppose you always have reams and reams of copying to do and never interrupt your copying to let people get on the machine who have just a few pages to do. Do you find people mumbling and complaining as they stand in line? Are people unwilling to do favors for you? By understanding how your actions affect people, you can modify your actions so they affect people as you want them to.

Recognize That There Are Different Ways People Can Respond to Your Actions.

Sometimes people can be quite direct: "You know, it's really a drag when I just have a few sheets to copy and you won't let me on the machine." Other times, their comments can be so subtle that you might miss them. Suppose you speak very haltingly and say "uh" a lot. Your listeners get tired of waiting for the next sentences to come, so they start fidgeting in their seats and talking with one another. Eventually your boss stops calling on you in meetings.

■■■

Putting All the Self-Awareness Factors Together

In this chapter, we've explored the many ways you can become fully aware of the wealth of information you have about who you are. We've looked at the roles your appraisals, senses, feelings, intentions, and actions play in providing you with that information. Take what you've learned about each one of the components of your self-awareness system, and put it all together in this exercise.

■■■

Exercise: Using the Five Self-Awareness Components

1. At the end of the day, sit back for a few minutes and recall some activity or task that you did. It could be a very simple one: going into Helen's office to talk with her.

2. Note how each of the five self-awareness components came into play. *I walked down to Helen's office to ask her a question* (intention). *I saw her typing fast and furiously on her computer* (senses) *and figured she must be very keen to finish the project* (appraisal). *I was very happy* (feeling) *she was working so hard. I didn't want to disturb her concentration* (intention), *so I slipped out of her office* (action).

3. Examine if any of the components are working at cross-purposes. In the example with Helen, the initial intention—to talk with her—was overruled by the recognition that she wasn't free to talk. So you altered your course of action, quite logically.

   But let's take another example. You decide to call one possible new customer (intention). As you are dialing his number, you feel your stomach clenching (senses). You realize that you are too nervous to make the call (interpretation). So you hang up the phone (action). You feel angry at yourself that you aren't able to make the call (feeling). Here your nervousness is definitely setting your actions at cross-purposes, sabotaging your ability to make the call.

4. Try to find ways to avoid having the components work at cross-purposes. In the preceding example, after hanging up the phone you might try a bit of affirming inner dialogue: *I'm a good salesperson. We have a good product, and I can tell the customer exactly why. I have had lots of success with other calls. If this person doesn't want the product, there are many other potential customers I can call.* Then you can try calling again.

■■■

You can see from this exercise that by tuning into all of the components of your self-awareness system, you get a full picture of a particular situation and are in a better position to choose the most effective course of action.

Another way you can practice tuning into all five components simultaneously is by asking yourself several times a day the following self-awareness questions: What am I feeling right now? What do I want? How am I acting? What appraisals am I making? What do my senses tell me?

As you've discovered in this chapter, developing high self-awareness requires practice and courage. In the process, you learn to step back and observe yourself in action and evaluate the course you are navigating. Next we see the many ways you can put to good use the information your self-awareness gives you. This begins in Chapter Two, with how self-awareness helps you manage your emotions.

2

Managing Your Emotions

We've all heard someone—maybe even ourselves—being admonished to "get in control of your emotions," or "chill out." We usually take this as meaning "stifle your emotions." But as we learned in Chapter One, emotions give us lots of clues as to why we do what we do. Stifling them deprives us of that information. Suppressing emotions also doesn't make them go away; it can leave them free to fester, as we've seen in the case of anger.

Managing your emotions means something quite different from stifling them. It means understanding them and then using that understanding to turn situations to your benefit. Let's say you're in a meeting and your boss resoundingly denigrates a suggestion you made. Then he says that if you'd stick to what you're supposed to be doing you wouldn't come up with such harebrained ideas. A spontaneous, unchecked response from you might be, "You stupid, insensitive idiot. If you stuck to what *you* are supposed to be doing you would see what a good idea it is!" While you might be quite right, such an outburst on your part will surely result in another severe reprimand, and perhaps even dismissal.

Here's the emotionally intelligent way of dealing with that situation. You first become aware that you are feeling anger. You then tune in to your thoughts. The first ones might not be so ennobling: *He's a pig. I could kill him.* But then you engage in a constructive internal dialogue: *He's being unreasonable. I will not sink to his level.*

I will not allow my anger to show. I know my idea's a good one. Then
you might tune in to all the physiological changes—fast breathing,
pounding heart—you are experiencing, and practice relaxation
techniques. You look at your anger actions—clenching your jaw,
making a fist—and stop doing them. Then you give yourself a few
minutes' time-out by leaving the room to get a cold drink of water.
Finally, after the meeting you seek a solution to this problem of your
boss's publicly putting you down.

In this chapter, we look at different ways you can learn to manage your emotions. We see how taking charge of your thoughts, vis-
ceral responses, and behavioral actions works to this end, and the
role that problem solving plays. Being aware of your emotions (as
we see in the example of checking your angry response) is the first
step. If need be, refer back to the section "Get in Touch with Your
Feelings" in Chapter One.

The Components of Your Emotional System Must Work Together

In my seminars, I often liken the emotions to a computer. In the
same way that your PC consists of different components (hard drive,
monitor, printer) that are interfaced with each other, your emotional system is made up of different components that interact and
must all work together and efficiently for optimum performance. If
the components fail to work as they should, the system can crash.

In the case of your emotions, the components are:

- Your thoughts or cognitive appraisals
- Your physiological changes or arousal actions
- Your behaviors or action tendencies

As to which component actually sets your emotional system in
motion, some argue that thoughts precede bodily changes, while others take the opposite position. There's a large group that believes

behavior comes before thoughts or physiological changes. I see no value in getting involved in this chicken-or-egg debate. What is important is to understand that emotions are produced by an interaction of these three components in response to an external event; by taking charge of them, we are able to effectively manage our emotions.

Actually, there is another component to your emotional system: your emotional context, or your emotional makeup. This encompasses how you were brought up, what you believe, experiences you have had—in fact, everything that makes you who you are today. It can be a fight you had with your wife before coming to work that causes you to feel depressed all day, childhood instructions to be nice and not challenge anyone that lead you to be passive and suppress anger and similar emotions, or the physical abuse you suffered at the hands of your father that causes you to feel perpetual anger with male bosses. Your emotional context underlies all three components of your emotional system and can influence your emotional responses to varying degrees.

Clearly it is well beyond the scope of this book to explore emotional context. I bring it up now because it can imbue a situation with an emotional undercurrent that challenges your emotional management system to the fullest. Understanding your emotional context (the subject of countless books and therapy sessions) is optimal, but the more focused solution here is to bring your emotional management tools into play in the workplace. You then deal with the manifestations—say, angry outbursts at your boss—not the context (your abusive relationship with your father).

In the next section, we look at how you can use the three components of your emotional system to manage your emotions effectively.

How to Make Your Thoughts, Physiological Changes, and Behaviors Work for You

It is important to keep in mind that it is your own thoughts, bodily changes, and behaviors that drive your emotional responses, not someone else's actions or an external event. In the example of the denigrating boss, it is your thoughts about your boss's outburst, your pounding heart, and your clenched fist that cause you to experience anger. By understanding this, you recognize that the power to manage your anger and indeed all your other emotions rests with you, not with your nasty boss or anyone else, and that managing your anger involves taking charge of the three components of your emotional system.

Take Charge of Your Thoughts

Your boss's reprimand generates a number of thoughts. *I could kill him* is one; *I know my idea's a good one* is another. We "hear" our thoughts by tuning into our inner dialogues (which we discussed in the first chapter under "Examine How You Make Appraisals"). These internal conversations, which may precede, accompany, or follow emotions, play an important part in defining and shaping our emotional experiences. For example, it's easy to see how the statement "I'm going to kill him" can only perpetuate your anger, whereas the different statement "I'll talk to my boss about this tomorrow" can help reduce your anger.

We often have the same inner dialogue over and over, as the situation repeats itself, thus causing us to engage in destructive internal dialogues as soon as the situation arises. Suppose your coworker repeatedly takes files out of your office but never puts them back, even though you've asked him on several occasions to do so. Your internal conversation might go something like this: *He's so selfish. He never listens to me. He's completely disrespectful. I can't stand this anymore.* Each time you look for a file that he hasn't put back, this counterproductive dialogue is triggered. Well, your coworker gradually picks up on this; then he begins feeling that you are a generally angry person, and that you dislike him.

The thoughts that spontaneously pop out (*I could kill him; He's so selfish*) are what we call "automatic thoughts." They are different from the internal dialogues we discussed under self-appraisal, which usually involve some deliberation (*I have all the facts at hand; the points are in order; I will make a fine presentation*). The latter we call inner dialogue or internal conversation. Taking charge of both kinds of thoughts is an important step in managing your emotions.

Tune in to Your Automatic Thoughts

Automatic thoughts usually share some characteristics:

THEY TEND TO BE IRRATIONAL.

Because they are spontaneous, they are uncensored. You can say something outrageous like "I'd like to kill him," even though you never in your life have seriously considered killing anyone. The intensity of the thought is a reflection of the intensity of your anger. Because they just pop out, you don't have time to consider the logic of the automatic thought. In the case of the coworker, you tend to make generalizations that aren't necessarily valid. "He never listens to me" is just not true; your problem with him is only over the files.

WE USUALLY BELIEVE THEM.

Automatic thoughts happen so fast that we generally don't question them. "He's always so disrespectful" comes into your head so often about your coworker that you just accept as truth that he's disrespectful.

THEY ARE OFTEN CRYPTIC.

Automatic thoughts are often expressed as a kind of short hand: "Jerk." "Liar." "I'm dead meat."

THEY TEND TO TRIGGER OTHER AUTOMATIC THOUGHTS.

As you can see in the case of the coworker with the files, one thought acts like a catalyst for another: "He's so selfish. He never listens to me. He's completely disrespectful. I hope he gets fired." This not only perpetuates and exacerbates your feeling of anger, but it makes it more difficult for you to shut off those thoughts; it's like the domino effect.

AUTOMATIC THOUGHTS CAN LEAD TO DISTORTED THINKING.

Take the instance of a boss who calls you in to her office to talk about her disappointment over the unsatisfactory relationship your client says he is having with you. Here are some examples of automatic thoughts that might flash through your mind:

"I'm in big trouble."

"She thinks I've really messed up."

"She's going to fire me."

"I won't be able to find another job."

"I'll lose everything."

"My family will leave me."

The emotion you're experiencing here is fear. But let's sit tight in this meeting with the boss a little longer. She seems visibly upset. You interpret her anger as being directed at you. You become defensive. But after you talk longer, you learn that your predecessor also had problems with the client, and your boss is losing her patience with the client, not with you. Because you went in to the meeting with insufficient information about the situation, your automatic thoughts jumped in with erroneous assessments.

The nature of distressful situations, such as being reprimanded by your boss or being annoyed by a coworker, is that they tend to generate distorted thinking: styles and patterns of thinking that color your perception of reality. Learning how to avoid distorted thinking helps you can gain greater control over your automatic thoughts and manage your emotions.

■■■

Tips for Avoiding Distorted Thinking

Don't Overgeneralize.

Statements such as "I'm always so slow to catch on" and "He never listens to me" come up because of specific circumstances. By generalizing, you give the wrong impression that the statements always apply. Yes, you were slow to catch on to an idea being presented, but you are usually very quick. The generalization here can only lead to feelings of low self-esteem. Yes, your coworker doesn't listen to you about the files, but he does listen about other things. The overgeneralization here can cause you to feel inappropriately indignant and morally superior—attributes that do not endear you to anyone. It is more accurate to say "sometimes" instead of "always" or "never."

Stay away from Destructive Labeling.

"She's a jerk." "He's so inconsiderate." Here again, your interpretations are based on specific situations. Yes, your boss behaved unfairly and disrespectfully toward you, but he doesn't always. So, too, with the coworker. By using this destructive labeling, you suggest to yourself that the situation is irrevocably bad, and there's nothing you can do to fix it.

Avoid Mind Reading.

We often don't know what another person's motives or intentions are. It's easy to see what unnecessary anxiety is caused by thinking that your boss is going to fire you. Assuming that your coworker doesn't respect you is also an example of trying to read minds. If you have questions about a situation (is your boss going to fire you? does your coworker not respect you?), hold off on drawing any conclusions until you have more information. Asking directly is sometimes a good way of getting the information: "You seem dissatisfied with my performance. Is this the case?"

Don't Have Rules About How Others Should Act.

This is what Plato called the "ought motive": "My boss ought to have apologized to me for how he treated me in the meeting." By having rules for how people should act, you set yourself up for much disappointment and anger because people very often don't behave as we want. We become convinced that injustice is being perpetrated. Not only that: such distorted thinking interferes with our ability to understand the other person (understanding others is a key ingredient of developing good relationships with them, as we see in Part Two of this book) because we see the other person from our own perspective. By recognizing that people are all different, knowing that they all have their own sets of rules, and being flexible and allowing for other people's ways of doing things, you automatically stay away from such words as *ought, should,* and *must.*

Don't Inflate the Significance of an Event.

Let's say you can't find a letter that the other party's attorney sent to your boss. You've searched everywhere for it, you feel certain that your boss did give it to you, and you know you should have copied it right away, but you didn't. You might say to yourself, *This is a catastrophe. I'm going to lose my job. We're going to lose the case. I can't bear it.* None of this is probably true, unless of course you repeatedly lose correspondence your boss gives you. The situation is bad, but it is far from a disaster. You can always call the other attorney and ask that the letter be sent again, although you might be somewhat embarrassed by having to do so. Turning the consequences of a negative event into a catastrophe means magnifying its intensity many times over. Instead of feeling mildly worried, you become seriously anxious, which only distorts your thinking even more. Avoid using such words as *catastrophe* and *disaster,* but if you do hear yourself saying them, be aware that your thoughts are magnifying the importance of the event. Don't say "I can't take this," because you *can* take it.

■■■

In the next section we look again at some of these same situations to see how carrying on constructive inner dialogues helps override the negative effects of automatic thoughts.

Develop Constructive Inner Dialogues

As we discussed earlier, the difference between automatic thoughts and inner dialogues is that the former are spontaneous and often counterproductive, whereas the latter are deliberate and can be productive. By avoiding automatic thoughts as much as possible, by cutting them off as soon as they start, and by learning how to have effective inner dialogues, you can help defuse the effects of distressful situations. You can even learn to reprogram some destructive automatic thoughts to avoid having them in the first place.

Take the example of your coworker's not returning the files. Here are some ways to manage your anger in this situation. Let's say the automatic thoughts (*He never listens to me* and so on) have already come to mind. First, acknowledge the emotion: "I'm really angry at Gerald." Then restate the generalization, "He never listens to me," so it applies just to the particular situation: "Gerald doesn't return the files when I ask him to do so." You can't say he doesn't listen to you (that would be mind reading) because maybe he does. He doesn't return the files because he's busy doing other things and forgets; or maybe he's holding on to them because he might need them again, but he neglected to tell you that.

Next, turn the destructive labeling "He's so inconsiderate" into a thought that again looks at the particular situation: "Gerald seems to be inconsiderate when he doesn't put the files put back in my office. But he often does very nice things for me in other situations." This thinking keeps you from seeing no possible solution (if Gerald were absolutely inconsiderate, there would be none, and this realization would make you angrier). Acknowledging Gerald's positive attributes makes it easier for you to be solution-oriented.

As for the automatic thought "He doesn't respect me," which suggests mind reading, if you're really concerned that Gerald doesn't respect you, you might say to yourself, "It makes me think that Gerald doesn't respect me, but I have no other indication that that's how he regards me. Maybe I'll ask him." This way, you can dismiss your presumption of lack of respect, whether because you see no evidence for it or because Gerald tells you that it's not so.

We've seen how saying "I can't stand this anymore" is counterproductive. An alternative inner dialogue that better covers that territory might go something like this: *This has happened so many times with Gerald, and it's making me angrier and angrier. I think I'll talk to him during coffee break and tell him that it's really hard for me when I need to have the files in my office yet I have to go chasing after them. I'll ask him if there's some way we could resolve this. I would even be willing to come and get the files if he called me as soon as he was done with them.* This is an example of problem solving (which we get into a little later on), but the point to remember is that instead of backing yourself into a corner, give yourself an action plan for resolving the problem.

Your inner dialogue can also take the form of questions: *Why do I get so furious with Gerald when I don't with Andre, who often does the same thing? Am I really so inconvenienced by not having the files? Or am I really angry with Gerald because he got the nicer cubicle?* By asking questions, you begin to explore the meaning of your emotions, and you can use this knowledge to help resolve the situation.

Another useful type of internal dialogue is the instructive statement, which helps guide you through emotionally stressful situations. Instructive statements reassure you and suggest the course you should follow. (Examples of such statements are in the exercise below.) Through my seminars, I've learned that people find it very helpful to prepare ready-to-use instructive statements for emotionally provoking situations they are likely to encounter. Here's an exercise for doing that.

■■■

Exercise to Prepare Sample Instructive Statements

1. Suppose that within the next three months you are likely to encounter three situations that promise to be emotionally volatile and cause you considerable stress. As illustrations, let's consider a job evaluation; a presentation of a report, plan, or idea; and a response to an angry client, customer, employee, or manager.

2. Taking one situation at a time, imagine the emotions it is likely to cause. Some possibilities are fear, anxiety, embarrassment, anger, and shame.

3. Write down instructive statements you can use to help you effectively manage your emotions in the situation.

Here are some examples. The first set relate to a performance evaluation:

"I have done a good job."

"I don't need to get defensive."

"I was not entirely satisfied with the outcome of (whatever), but the boss knows I had no control over the cause of the problem."

"In any case, overall I have worked very hard and gotten good results."

"I will try to learn from my boss how I can do better."

"If I don't understand what my boss is referring to, I will ask for specific examples."

"I will pay attention to the positive things she says, not just the negative ones."

Examples that relate to a presentation:

"I have fully prepared for this."

"I have all my notes at hand."

"I know my idea (or plan or report) is a sound one."

"I know the staff (or audience) will recognize what a thorough job I've done."

"I will speak slowly and clearly and look at people."

"I will do fine, and I will enjoy the presentation."

The third set of examples prepare you for an angry confrontation:

"I will listen carefully to what (whoever) says."

"I won't interrupt."

"I will speak slowly and calmly."

"I will acknowledge the other person's concerns."

"I will ask questions when something is unclear."

"I will ask the person how we might resolve the situation together."

Now repeat the exercise for three situations that you are *in fact* likely to face shortly.

It is easy to see that by preparing yourself with such instructive statements, you have a much better chance of handling the situation in an emotionally intelligent manner. You are also well on your way to cutting off those negative automatic thoughts before they even start.

■■■

Emotional Intelligence at Work

As my company's press relations person, I have to do about thirty press conferences a year. They used to cause me tremendous anxiety for days beforehand. Then I started to explore my thoughts and found that I had been telling myself that I wouldn't make a good showing, I didn't know what I was talking about, I would be ridiculed. No wonder I was so anxious!

Then, whenever I started to feel anxious, I would take a few deep breaths and ask, "What am I telling myself? What am I uptight about?" I found that most of the things didn't make sense—I would never be ridiculed. The things that did make sense—like I really didn't know the material well enough—caused me to get better prepared.

Now, a week before each press conference I tell myself over and over, "It's going to be great. I'm well prepared. It's an opportunity to educate the press. I won't look foolish." I can honestly tell you that I now look forward to press conferences. (Dennis M., press officer for a high-tech company)

■■■

Manage Your Arousal

The next component of the emotional system is arousal, or physiological changes. You will recall that in Chapter One, on self-awareness, we discussed how feelings tend to be associated with specific physical sensations: nervousness with a jittery stomach, anger with warm cheeks. We explored how you can often get in touch with your feelings by looking at both their sensory and behavioral manifestations. Here we look at the physiological changes behind those sensations—what we also refer to as arousal. We explore how you can tune in to the changes and use them as a cue that it's time to calm yourself to a level of arousal that enables you to think and act effectively.

How to Identify Shifts in Arousal

Increases in heart rate, blood pressure, respiration rate, and perspiration rate are all signs of physiological changes. They may be associated with any number of different emotions; the first step is not to identify which one, but to acknowledge that a change in your arousal level has indeed taken place.

Let's say you're sitting at your desk going over your recent sales figures, and they look pretty good. You're feeling pleased and proud. Then you get a call from your boss: "Carla, I have some bad news." You feel your heart beating faster. "St. Mary's Hospital has decided to go with Sansome Pharmaceuticals instead of us." You feel your breath coming more quickly, perspiration beading on your forehead. Your arousal level has gone from a calm state to a heightened one. The emotions associated with the changes here are probably anxiety (when your boss says she has bad news) and fear (St. Mary's was your major customer, and without them you have no chance of achieving adequate sales goals).

By instantly noting the physiological changes, you give yourself the opportunity to use them as a cue that it's time to modify them. (We look at some techniques for doing that in the next section.) By modifying the changes, you can diminish the anxiety and fear, and thus keep them from becoming overwhelming. Remember, it's much easier to prevent yourself from getting anxious or angry than it is to stop those emotions once they have taken over.

By not tuning in to the changes in your arousal level, you run the risk of acting impulsively. For instance, your boss says she has some bad news and you immediately let forth an expletive you will later regret. She tells you what St. Mary's has decided and you begin yelling: "How could those idiots at St. Mary's do that? I always knew they couldn't be counted on." Or you say to yourself, "This is it. I'm going to get fired. I can't handle this." All of these impulses can have unfortunate consequences. The expletive suggests to your boss that you can't handle difficult situations. Calling the people at St. Mary's idiots gives her a clue as to why the hospital went with another supplier. Your comments to yourself only serve to engender and exacerbate anxiety, fear, and anger, all of which show.

Here's an explanation of why these changes take place. Humans are programmed with a fight-or-flight response for coping with stressful situations. Originally it was designed to ensure survival. (You're foraging in the woods and come across a saber-toothed tiger; you flee. You come across a member of a clan with whom your clan is competing for territory, and you fight.) Your heart rate increases and more blood flows to your brain, organs, muscles, and other parts of the body so they have more nutrients and can respond best, whether you fight or flee. Your breathing rate increases so that more oxygen is brought to all parts of your body, because oxygen is what your cells need to work.

As you can see, the fight-or-flight response is very useful for life-or-death situations, when you need that massive infusion of blood and oxygen. But these aren't the kind of situation we face in our usual workday (though it sometimes seems that way). Frequent increases in heart or breathing rate can actually take a toll on our bodies, by causing a number of adverse physiological problems, from hypertension to heart attack. So our physical health is just another reason why we want to keep changes in our arousal to a comfortable level. Here's an exercise for learning how you can recognize changes in your arousal level so as to manage your arousal.

∎∎∎

Exercise for Tuning into Changes in Your Arousal Level

1. At the beginning of each day, over a two-week period, choose two situations you will experience during that particular day (they don't need to be the same ones each day), one of which is likely to have no effect on your arousal level, the other of which is likely to result in a marked increase in your arousal level. Make sure that prior to and during these situations you do not consume anything that could affect your heart rate, as do coffee, caffeinated soda pops, sugared products, cigarettes, and other stimulants. Also, choose situations that you expect to result in different emotional responses, so you can become familiar with the physiological changes associated with each one.

2. While the situation is taking place, try to pay careful attention to your breathing, your heart rate, and whether or not you are perspiring. This is especially difficult in stressful situations, as your attention is focused on the situation itself; but make an effort.

3. Immediately after each situation, write down what your heart rate, breathing rate, and perspiration were like. Here are examples:

Situation	Heart Rate	Breathing Rate	Perspiration
typing invoices	slow	slow and regular	none
speaking in meeting	fast	fast and irregular	beads on forehead

Because the arousal level can vary so markedly, from an emotionally inert state (like that created by typing invoices) to an emotionally active one (speaking in a meeting), even by the end of the first week you will become quite adept at instantly tuning in to changes in your arousal level. Once you can do that, you are ready to learn how to diminish your arousal.

∎∎∎

Use Relaxation to Decrease Your Arousal

We've learned how to tune into changes in our arousal level so we can notice them immediately. The next step is to diminish the arousal as soon as we discern it. The most effective way of doing so is by relaxing. When you relax, you slow down such bodily activities as breathing and pumping blood and restore your body to its normal state. This then slows down your emotional response, giving you time to determine the best course of action to take.

There are many ways to learn relaxation techniques. Meditation, yoga, self-hypnosis, and biofeedback are just a few. Different ones work for different people. Here we learn a conditioned relaxation response, one that doesn't require reading another book or taking a class to learn.

The premise behind the conditioned relaxation response is that you first associate relaxation with specific images and thoughts. Then, whenever you are in a distressful situation, you call up those images and thoughts to relax you. Soon you begin to associate the distressful situations with the calming images and thoughts. Eventually, the first signs of a stressful situation call up those images and thoughts, and you relax. The result is that the period of emotional distress is shortened considerably. Here are the steps for learning the response.

■■■

Exercise for Developing a Conditioned Relaxation Response

1. Choose an appropriate place to practice: a calm, quiet place where you will not be disturbed or distracted. This prevents stimuli or events (noise in the corridor, your phone ringing) from disturbing you as you concentrate on relaxing images and thoughts.

2. Find a comfortable position. (If your leg becomes cramped or your back starts to hurt, you will lose your concentration; so find some position that you can comfortably hold during the course of the practice.) It might be lying against the pillows on your bed, or sitting on a sofa. The goal is to reduce all muscular tension.

3. Adopt a passive attitude. Passivity is probably the most important component in developing your conditioned relaxation response, because when you are passive, you're not bothered. You just let things happen; you relax. To achieve passivity, you might engage in an internal dialogue something like this: *If something distracts me, that's OK, it just means I need to learn better how to tune the distractions out. If this response seems hard to do, that's OK, it just means I need to practice it more. Whatever happens when I'm practicing, that's OK, I'll just let it happen.*

4. Choose a calming mental construct that works for you, and repeat it to yourself over and over. This can be an image (a calm lake), a word (*peace*), a sound (*shhhh*), a statement (*I am at rest*)—whatever feels comfortable to you. Then imagine it, say it, or sound it out over and over. This helps you shift your mind from being externally oriented to internally oriented, so you keep yourself from distraction by external factors. Spend about twenty minutes each day doing this, concentrating hard on whatever image or sound you have chosen. Eventually, someone could be shouting on the street below and you won't even hear it because you'll be so focused on the image of the calm lake, or the sound *shhhh*. I have found that by practicing twenty minutes each day, most people can develop the conditioned relaxation response in ten to fourteen days.

■■■

Once you have conditioned yourself to relax at will, you can use your relaxation response to short-circuit any change in arousal. Here's how you do that.

■■■

Exercise for Learning to Use Your Conditioned Relaxation Response

1. Choose a distressful situation that you are likely to encounter in your everyday work, one that causes a particular emotion. This

can be making a cold call (anxiety), confronting a coworker about a problem (anger), or talking about a possible job layoff (depression)—whatever is appropriate in your job situation.

2. Imagine yourself in that situation. Use all your senses. In your mind, go through the steps you are likely to take in the situation (with the cold call, this means looking up the phone number, dialing the number, asking for the person, introducing yourself) and try to evoke any sensations or behavioral actions you might experience (fast heartbeat, rapid breathing, quiet voice, shaky speech).

3. Introduce your mental construct into the imagined situation. As you go through each of the steps of the process in your mind and anticipate the accompanying sensory or behavior response, tune into your relaxation image, sound, or statement. For example, as you imagine asking for the person and your voice quivering, say to yourself, *peace . . . peace . . . peace . . .,* or imagine the calm lake, or do whatever you have chosen as your mental construct.

4. Repeat this whole process once a day for several days. Each time, use the same situation and the same emotion (you'll work on others once you have mastered this one). When you are able to automatically shift, almost instantly, from the first signs of a change in arousal to your relaxation construct, you have learned to associate your mental construct with the distressful situation. You're ready to move on to using your conditioned relaxation response in the real situation.

5. Introduce the mental construct into the real situation. Go through all of the stages involved in making an actual cold call. At the first sign of a change in arousal, instantly call up your chosen image, word, sound, or statement. The ultimate goal is to have the image, word, or sound kick in just before any changes in arousal occur. If you find it is too difficult, then go back to practicing in the imagined situation until you can successfully use the technique in the real situation.

■■■

What you are doing here is reprogramming your arousal for calmness so that it is easier for you to think and act effectively. Now let's look at how to take control of your behavior to achieve the same end.

Take Control of Your Behavioral Patterns

Behavioral patterns are actions that you tend to do over and over in response to a particular situation. For example, perhaps you yell when you get angry, tap your pencil on the desk when anxious, smile when pleased. Just as our physiological changes are tied closely to our emotions, the same is true of our behaviors. So to manage our emotions, we need to be able to take control of our behaviors; to do that, we must first be able to recognize them.

Learn to Recognize Your Behaviors

Certain behaviors are generally associated with specific emotions. For example, we approach people when we are enthusiastic, we sit around doing little when we are depressed, and we fidget when we are nervous. As we've seen with physiological changes, when you allow them to go unchecked they perpetuate the emotion. If you don't use relaxation to decrease your heart beat or slow down your breathing, you perpetuate your anger. The same is true here. By allowing yourself to go on fidgeting, you can't help yourself lessen your anxiety.

Often, we don't notice our own behaviors. We've raised our voice in response to anger for so long that we're not even aware that we do it. Here's an exercise to help you tune in to your behaviors.

■■■

Exercise for Recognizing Your Behaviors

1. Make a list of emotions. In a notebook, write a number of emotions that you are likely to experience in your workplace. Here are some examples:

Anger

Joy

Anxiety

Contentment

Depression

Enthusiasm

Fear

Confidence

Sadness

Frustration

2. Monitor the emotions, and see what behavioral patterns accompany them. During a two-week period, monitor each of the emotions on your list and the accompanying behavioral actions. Let's say you are afraid the chief engineer is going to move you to another site. As a result, you avoid passing her office, you sit as far from her as you can in the lunchroom, and you skip a meeting that she is going to be at. To take another example, suppose you have just been given the go-ahead for a project and are feeling confident. You tell your coworkers about it somewhat boastfully. For all of the emotions on the list, note the corresponding behavioral actions.

3. Look for any patterns. Let's take the example of a possible move. You're afraid that you might be moved to another site, but you also fear that your coworker told your boss that last week, when you said you had a dentist appointment, you really went to the ball game. You respond by doing everything you can to avoid running into your boss or your coworker. Looking at your behavioral actions in response to these two fearful instances, you probably deduce that when you're afraid you avoid the people who are connected to your fear. (We discuss how you can use this knowledge in the next section.)

4. Ask others for input here. If you feel comfortable, you might want to ask a coworker who knows you well and respects you, or your

assistant—probably not your boss—how you react when you're angry, anxious, or depressed. For example, your coworker might tell you he's noticed that when you get frustrated that things aren't going anywhere in meetings you tend to get sarcastic, making comments like "Well that suggestion should certainly win you a MacArthur award."

■■■

By the end of two weeks, you should begin to have a good picture of how you act when you are experiencing a number of different emotions. Now we look at how you can use that information to work to your benefit.

Derail Counterproductive Behaviors

As you can probably imagine from these examples, sarcasm, avoidance, and boastfulness are counterproductive behaviors. Sarcasm alienates the people it is directed against, avoidance makes your boss and coworker think you're being rude, and boastfulness makes your coworkers not want to talk with you. Here are some ways you can derail those behaviors that work against you.

■■■

Tips for Staying on Top of Your Behavioral Actions

1. Take deep breaths. This might seem rather futile when you've got something as forceful as rage behind you, but deep breathing serves several functions. First of all, it keeps you from doing anything else. If you're concentrating on taking deep breaths, you're not going to be able to yell or go off bragging to coworkers. Second, it's a signal to yourself: pay attention, get control, stop doing what you're doing. Third, deep breathing slows you down.

2. Engage in a constructive inner dialogue. In the earlier section on taking charge of your thoughts, we saw how useful internal dialogues can be in helping to get clarity, refocus, and alter your

course of action. They serve a similar function here. Let's say you have recognized that you are afraid of the possible site transfer. You have identified your corresponding behavior as being avoidance. Here's a constructive internal dialogue for this situation:

VOICE #1: I'm afraid of being transferred to another site, and what I am doing is hiding from the chief engineer.

VOICE #2: Am I gaining anything from this behavior?

VOICE #1: Well, by not talking with her I'm delaying finding out the bad news. On the other hand, the news might be good—maybe I won't be transferred. In any case, I'm just prolonging and intensifying my fearfulness.

VOICE #2: The chief engineer probably thinks I don't like her, or I don't want to have anything to do with her, or I'm a bit peculiar.

VOICE #1: I'm wasting a lot of time with this cat-and-mouse game.

VOICE #2: What would work better for me here?

You might decide that you should ask the chief engineer if you could meet with her for a few minutes. Then you tell her that you have heard rumors that you're going to be transferred to another site, and you're wondering if there is any truth to the rumor. This comes under problem solving, our next point of discussion.

■■■

Become a Good Problem Solver

The basis of good management is effective problem-solving skills: determining the best way to get employees to work well together, figuring out how to get the staff behind a new project, and so on. This is true whether you're managing a staff or managing your emotions.

Generally, a distressful emotion is caused by a problem situation: the lost attorney letter, the possible site transfer, the coworker who doesn't return files. To effectively manage your emotions, you need to develop good problem-solving skills, the goal being to determine the most effective course of action to take to resolve the problem. But before we explore some ways you can become a good problem solver, you need first to understand the nature of problems.

If you think of life as a series of situations that require some kind of response, then no situation is inherently a problem. It is the ineffectiveness of your response that makes it so. Take the case of the lost attorney letter. You look for it in your desk, your briefcase, next to the copy machine, but you can't find it. The lost letter is not the problem (because if you found it there wouldn't be a problem), but your inability to find it is. Your ineffective response to the situation of the lost letter is causing the problem.

This is not an exercise in semantics. The value of looking at problems this way is first to see that they constitute a normal part of life. After all, we can't possibly always choose the most effective way of handling a situation, and this means we create problems. Second, if your initial response to a situation is not working—you can't find the letter—then you always have the option of choosing another response (ask someone to help you look, or call the attorney to ask for another letter).

Once you accept that problems are a normal part of life, then you no longer go on thinking there is something wrong with you for having them. You are also less likely to deny that they even exist. We tend to deny problems because they usually upset us, but denying them doesn't make them go away. Figuring out how best to resolve the situation that brought on the problem is how to make the problem go away; that's problem solving. Here are ways you can learn to develop good problem-solving skills.

Identify and Define the Problem Situation

When you state a problem specifically and concretely, you put it in focus and force yourself to see what is relevant and what isn't. Let's say you state the problem situation this way: "My job is driving me nuts." The abstract statement gives you no clues as to what specifically provokes you, why it happens, or who is involved. Thus any resolution is quite elusive. The emotionally intelligent way of identifying the problem situation is to define the specific irritants. You ask yourself who, what, why, when, how. These might be some answers to understanding why your job is driving you nuts: "I am given much too much work to do. My boss is in over his head, so he's not there for me. My coworkers don't seem to know what they should be doing, so they're not doing much of anything. I'm always frustrated and tired." Once you clearly define the problem situation, you can look at it differently.

Change Your Perception of the Situation

One of the difficulties with problem situations is that we tend to look at them with tunnel vision. We get stuck in our usual mode of dealing with things, and then we can't find a solution. By reframing our thoughts about the situation, we are able to come up with new and useful responses. Here are some reframing thoughts:

- The real problem isn't who is involved; the real problem is how I respond.

- The real problem isn't what's done that bothers me; the real problem is how I feel.

- The real problem isn't how it happens; the real problem is when I deal with it.

- The real problem isn't why it happens; the real problem is why I respond the way I do.

Here are some ways to reframe thoughts about the dreadful job:

- The real problem isn't my boss and coworkers, but the fact that I never talk to them about the difficulties I'm having.

- The real problem isn't that my boss keeps giving me more and more work, but that I haven't found a way to get help with it.

- The real problem isn't that my job is dreadful, but that it makes me feel frustrated, tired, angry, and depressed.

- The real problem isn't that my job is driving me crazy, but that I haven't yet found an effective way of dealing with the situation.

As you can see, reframing your thoughts about a problem situation enables you to look at the situation afresh. You can then see that you're no longer stuck in a rut but simply facing a challenging situation for which you're on your way to finding an effective response. The way to do that is to look at a variety of options.

Generate Alternative Solutions

The goal here is to come up with half a dozen different strategies, because a generous number of options gives you the best chance of finding the most effective solution. Brainstorming is one of the most useful methods for coming up with a number of creative solutions. The idea behind brainstorming is that you toss out ideas as fast as they come to you. In brainstorming, *storm* is the keyword: just let the torrent of ideas flow, unedited, uncensored. Here are some ways to have a productive brainstorming session.

■■■

Tips for Effective Brainstorming

1. Defer judgment. Don't start criticizing ideas during a brainstorming session, as that inhibits further flow of ideas. Just write the thoughts down as fast as they come, and defer judging their merits until the decision-making stage.

2. Encourage freewheeling thinking. The wilder the idea, the better, because it's the very craziness that opens you up to all kinds of

imaginative solutions. Besides, it's easier to tame a wild idea than to make a creative solution out of a lame idea.

3. Go for quantity. The more ideas, the more options you have. The more ideas you propose, the more new ones you come up with.

4. Leave the details for later. Just come up with the broad ideas; you can fill in the specifics after you've generated your list. Defining the details impedes your brainstorming.

5. Use ideas as catalysts for others. Combine ideas, build upon ideas, come up with opposite ideas—anything to keep them coming.

■■■

Explore Different Options

Here are a few ideas that might have been on your brainstorming list in the instance of the dreadful job:

- Find another job.
- Take one sick day a week.
- Find some time to chill out.
- Don't do any work on the weekend.
- Give boss a lesson in management skills.
- Take time-management class.
- Suggest to boss we keep track of all hours we each spend on each project.
- Lead insurrection and take over department.
- Talk to Personnel about firing all do-nothing employees.
- Break down jobs I do into individual tasks and ask boss if others on staff can take over some.

Clearly, some of these ideas are wholly impractical. But you can see how they inspire others that are actually quite reasonable. Taking a sick day each week, though not a feasible solution, suggests another idea: that you need time to chill out. This one then leads to the idea of not doing any work on the weekend.

Look at each idea individually and carefully consider the consequences of implementing it. Take, for instance, the idea of giving your boss a lesson in management skills. Not a good idea, because your boss would probably see you as impertinent and arrogant—or itching for his job. But this idea leads to the one of your taking a time-management class, which is a sound one. Imagine yourself asking your boss if the company would pay for you to take a time-management class because you think it might help you cope better with the overwhelming amount of work you have. You might even imagine your boss also taking the class—you could let him seem to come up with the idea instead of you—or at least your sharing with him some of the things you learn, which will ultimately help him be a better manager.

Define the Best Strategies

Eliminate ideas that seem to be ineffective, and combine ideas if it's useful to do so. Then make a separate list of the three best strategies. Under each one, list as many of the positive and negative consequences of the strategy as you can. Here are helpful questions to ask yourself:

- How would this strategy affect what I need, what I want, and how I feel?

- How would it affect the people I work with?

- How would it affect the significant people in my life?

- What are its short-term consequences? Long-term consequences?

Let's apply some of these questions to exploring the benefits and drawbacks of the proposed strategy of not doing any work on the weekend. Here are some answers you might derive.

- It would give me time to chill out and be with my family.

- I'll probably have to work late several nights a week to get all the work done.

- It will help me feel less depressed, angry, and anxious.

- Because I'll be working late several nights, the other employees and my boss will see how diligent I am, and maybe it will inspire them to be more so.

- My family will miss me during the week, but they'll be assured I'll be with them the whole weekend.

- Because the boss sees that I'm no longer working on weekends, he probably won't ask me to do those week-end trade shows that take place three times a year, which I like attending.

It certainly seems that the benefits outweigh the drawbacks, so this would be a good strategy to implement. The second and third strategies you come up with might be to take a time-management class and to see how you can bring other staff members into your projects to do some of the tasks that you normally do. Carry out the same weighing of benefits and drawbacks with those strategies.

Evaluate the Results

You now have three strategies for coping with the situation of the horrid job. Your problem-solving skills enable you to come up with a new response to a persistently irritating and distressing situation. But problem solving doesn't end there: the final stage is evaluating the results to see if you need to refine or alter your strategies. Here are some questions to ask yourself in this regard:

- Are things happening as I thought they would?

- Are the results meeting my goals?

- Is this solution better than the old one?

Let's say you are getting far behind in your work because you aren't working weekends, so far behind that you resume going in on weekends. This causes problems with your family, and it deprives you of the period of rest you need. You may have to go through the problem-solving process again to find a different solution: talk to your boss about getting even more help from the other members of the department; see if there's any way of scaling down some of the projects, and so on.

Additional Techniques for Managing Your Emotions

We've learned how to take charge of each of the three components of our emotional system, and we've seen the role of problem solving. Next we look at three additional techniques—using humor, redirecting your emotional energy, and taking time out—that you can use to help manage your emotions.

Use Humor

You've heard the adage that humor is the best medicine. You've undoubtedly experienced humor's salubrious effects on such negative emotions as anger, depression, sadness, and anxiety. Well, there's actually a scientific explanation for this phenomenon. Laughter, a by-product of humor, stimulates the release of protein substances called endorphins. As the level of endorphins in the brain increases, the perception of pain—whether physical or emotional—decreases. Essentially, laughter causes the body to produce its own painkiller.

There is of course another benefit to laughter: it serves as a distraction, turning us away—even for a moment—from whatever distressful emotion we may be having. It's a little difficult to be depressed about your awful job during the very moment that you're having a good laugh. That moment of respite can be quite useful in giving you pause to reappraise your situation, get control of your behavioral actions, or whatever. Here are some ways I've found to bring humor into my day.

■■■

Tips for Generating Humor

1. Put on "Candid Camera" glasses. Take five or ten minutes out of your workday and try looking at your coworkers, your office, and your boss through a hidden-camera perspective, as in the old TV program of the same name. Observe them from an absurd, whimsical, or silly perspective, rather than the serious, somber, stomach-churning perspective from which you may normally view them. Moments ago, Edward was giving his usual lame excuses for why he couldn't help you out with the report; now he looks like a court jester holding forth at the water cooler. The reception area looks the cockpit from the starship *Enterprise,* with all its flashing lights and equipment. Your boss, moments before, was haranguing you about the report being late; she now looks like a silly magpie as she flits from office to office. Chances are that after this experience you'll return to your office feeling better disposed toward your boss, Edward, and the report. The point is not to laugh at others, but to gain awareness that we often take ourselves and the events we encounter too seriously.

2. Take a humor meditation break. When things get especially distressful during the day, try to take a short break of five or ten minutes to do something that is likely to produce a laugh, even a teeny one. Close your mind to external distractions as much as possible, and read funny passages from a joke book or humor scrapbook; look at the funnies in the newspaper; or think of a funny experience from the past.

3. Create a humor-filled environment. Set up a bulletin board in your office or workspace for cartoons, silly photographs, jokes, and humorous quotations. Then look at it whenever you need to laugh. Change its contents regularly so the humor stays fresh.

■■■

Redirect Your Emotional Energy

As you experience an intense emotion, energy is being expended. You tend to tense muscles and move your body more. Your circulatory and respiratory systems work much faster. Your mind goes at a quicker pace, with those automatic thoughts. What I've found works well in these situations is to redirect this energy into some activity that has nothing to do with the situation at hand.

Suppose you're extremely anxious about your job evaluation, which is to take place later in the day. You find yourself fidgeting and pacing, thinking *I'm going to get fired. He's going to give me a terrible evaluation.* Instead of continuing to fidget, pace, and entertain dreadful thoughts—which we've seen just perpetuate your anxiety—take up some simple task, some busywork. This distracts you from your anxiety and also helps you gain a sense of accomplishment that you're actually getting something useful done.

I find it's quite helpful if I make a list of some of these tasks—filing, ordering supplies, dusting, copying notes, cleaning my desk—and then pull out the list when I need some distracting busywork. Knowing there are constructive things you can do when you are angry or anxious is a good antidote to feeling immobilized by those emotions.

Take Time Out

In the same way that relaxation techniques can calm down your arousal level, taking a break from an emotionally taxing situation can slow down your emotional responses. Sometimes the time-out can be almost momentary: you take three deep breaths before responding to your angry boss. A brief time-out gives you the moment you need to keep yourself from saying something you might regret. Deep breaths are the first form of time-out you should practice.

Some situations may be so intense, so emotionally distressing, so potentially volatile that the only way to preserve your dignity (and perhaps even your job) is to remove yourself entirely. Recall the earlier example of your boss denigrating you in a meeting. Although it would be difficult to leave the meeting for an extended time-out (say, more than five minutes), you could excuse yourself to go to the bathroom. There you might dab some water on your neck or wrists to cool yourself down.

Suppose a coworker accosts you in the corridor and starts berating you for undermining his position with your mutual manager. You might say, "Look, this is really important, and I want to talk with you about this, but just let me go tell my assistant to hold my calls." This gives you a few moments to calm yourself down and collect your thoughts.

Anger is perhaps the most potentially volatile of all our emotions as it is usually another person who provokes our anger and at whom it is directed. With anger, you may need an extended time-out of an hour or more to return to a state in which it is possible to effectively deal with the situation. Here are some ways to defuse your anger.

■■■

Tips for Managing Your Anger

1. Communicate your anger. Let the person with whom you are having an angry exchange know that you are angry or that your stress is building. You might say something like, "I am beginning to feel very angry."

2. State your wish to remove yourself temporarily from the situation. You could say, "I would like to stop arguing for a little while so I can think more clearly. Then I'd like to get back together with you in an hour and talk this thing through." You should set a limit for the time-out, probably no more than an hour. (Leaving the time limit open-ended makes it too tempting to avoid the problem indefinitely, perhaps with the hope that it will resolve itself—which it won't.) Also, you don't want to put the other party at an unfair disadvantage by leaving it at your discretion what time you reconvene.

3. Remove yourself immediately. Then do some deep breathing, or use constructive self-statements in the time you have to yourself.

4. Use the time-out productively. During the time-out, do some useful busywork, as discussed above. Use your relaxation response
   to calm yourself.

■■■

Part Two explores how you can use your emotional intelligence
in dealing with others; there we discuss further how you and this
angry person might proceed to resolve the situation. For now, these
tips suffice to take you from a highly charged state to a considerably
calmer one, which, of course, is the goal of managing your emotions.

Even Positive Emotions Need to Be Managed

Although the emphasis in this chapter is on managing what might
be called negative emotions—anger, anxiety, fear, depression, frustration, and others—let me point out that such positive emotions
as joy, contentment, and confidence must also be managed.

For example, as nice as it sounds, enthusiasm can sometimes lead
to impulsive behavior. Think of a project proposed in a meeting that
you find so exciting it causes you to volunteer to head it up—even
though you already have more on your plate than you can handle.
Or the joy you feel over a promotion, which causes you to go around
boasting to your colleagues—one of whom was rejected for it.

It's easy to see that by using your emotional management techniques you can handle such situations more effectively. You might
take a few deep breaths and conduct a brief internal dialogue (*Slow
down. Don't do anything rash. This is a great idea. I would love to do it.
But I have much too much to do already.* And: *Calm down. Collect yourself. This promotion is great news. I can't wait to tell the others about it.*)
Then you might do a little problem solving: *This new project would be
a feather in my cap, and great fun, but it would take too much time and
would interfere adversely with my other projects. I won't volunteer to do
it. But if it still hasn't been done when I clear some things off my agenda,
then I'll see about doing it.* And: *If I boast about this promotion to the others, they'll think I'm being insensitive to Randi, who didn't get the job. And*

they may also worry about me getting too big for my britches. I'll leave it to my manager to notify the rest of the staff about my promotion.

It probably won't surprise you to learn that in my seminars I'm almost never asked how to manage happiness or confidence. But I hope you can see from such examples the value of applying your emotional management techniques to positive emotions just as you do to the negative ones.

Putting All the Emotional Management Tools Together

In this chapter, we've looked at the three components of your emotional system—your thoughts, physiological changes, and behavioral actions—and seen how staying on top of them is essential if you are to effectively manage your emotions. We've seen how these components interact with one another and work together: constructive internal thoughts can help slow down your physiological changes and behavioral actions, a diminished arousal level can help you gain control of your thoughts and behaviors, and productive behavioral responses such as deep breathing can help defuse destructive automatic thoughts and facilitate return to a comfortable arousal level. And we've also learned some extraordinarily useful methods for managing emotions, whether it's relaxation techniques or constructive inner dialogues, time-outs or problem solving.

As I said in the Introduction, emotional intelligence is the ability to intentionally make your emotions work for you. We've clearly seen in this chapter how managing your emotions is a key element. In the next chapter we explore another important ingredient of emotional intelligence: self-motivation. Managing your emotions is about staying on top of your emotions, but self-motivation has to do with getting *under* your emotions and using them to keep you focused, inspired, and moving ahead. Self-motivation draws upon many of the skills you've already learned, such as being able to recognize different emotions, engage in constructive internal dialogues, and use arousal and behaviors. In mastering these skills, you're ready to move on.

3

Motivating Yourself

We've all seen dozens of job announcements in which one of the qualifications sought in the applicant is self-motivation. The ad might say "Must be a good self-starter" or "Must work well on own," meaning that the person must be able to take on a task or job, stick with it, move ahead with it, and deal with any setbacks. It's easy to see why self-motivation is such a desirable attribute in the workplace: a self-motivated employee requires less management, has less downtime, and is likely to be more productive and creative.

Motivation Is the Key to Starting a Task and Staying with It

Technically, motivation is expending energy in a specific direction for a specific purpose. In the context of emotional intelligence, it means using your emotional system to catalyze the whole process and keep it going. Suppose you have a report to write and you're having a very hard time getting yourself to do it. You call your mother to chat, you head to the cafeteria for your sixth cup of coffee, and you dust off your recently dusted computer.

As an emotionally intelligent person, though, you recognize that what's missing in this picture is self-motivation. So you give yourself some motivationally instructive statements: *I've done plenty of reports. I can do this one with my eyes closed. I can do what it takes to get it done*. You walk briskly to the mailroom—even though you don't really need to go there—expressly to energize yourself. You give yourself a few little tasks related to the report, such as getting all your notes and documentation together. If motivation still eludes you, you call upon a supportive colleague, ostensibly for advice but really more to help you get back on track. You even summon in your mind your emotional mentor, Eleanor Roosevelt, for inspiration. You look around your office at the motivational objects you have placed there. Before long, you notice that your confidence and enthusiasm are returning. You're able to sit down at your very well-dusted computer and start writing. And somehow the report just seems to flow from your fingers.

In this chapter, we look carefully at the four sources you can draw upon for motivation: yourself; supportive friends, family, and colleagues; an emotional mentor; and your environment. Because we must sometimes face drastic situations that tend to wreak havoc with our motivation—cancellation of a project, loss of a promotion, or a job—we also explore how to deal with setbacks and create comebacks.

How people choose to utilize these sources of motivation and cope with setbacks differs from individual to individual, but the elements of motivation are common to us all: confidence, optimism, tenacity, enthusiasm, and resiliency. Confidence enables us to believe we have the capabilities to accomplish a task; optimism gives us hope that a positive resolution will ensue; tenacity keeps us focused on the task; enthusiasm allows us to enjoy the process; and resiliency enables us to start all over again. As we go through this chapter, we see how each of these elements is bolstered by the four sources of motivation and how it is only when these elements are working in tip-top form that our motivation is sufficient to get the job done.

Sources of Motivation

Finding yourself without motivation can be a distressing situation. You might feel isolated, frustrated, afraid, depressed, anxious. Your self-esteem probably takes a nosedive. The good news is that not only do you have available sources of motivation that you can draw upon to restore your motivation, but in the previous chapters you have already learned some useful techniques and tools for effectively dealing with waning motivation.

As I've just mentioned, there are four sources of motivation:

- Yourself (your thoughts, arousal, behaviors; all of these should be familiar concepts by now)

- Supportive friends, family, and colleagues (what I like to call your "A-team")

- An emotional mentor (a real or fictitious person)

- Your environment (the air, light, sounds, and messages in your office)

Although sometimes only one of these entities is necessary to build or revive your motivation, other situations may require the whole panoply. In the following sections, you learn how to draw upon each one, the goal being to use these sources of motivation to generate forces of motivation.

Yourself

You are the most powerful of the four sources of motivation (and conversely, of demotivation) because you are where it all begins. An individual (your colleague down the hall), an emotional mentor or inspirational hero (Emma Peel of *The Avengers*), or your environment (the photos around your office) can certainly boost your motivation, but it is ultimately your thoughts, your arousal, and your behavior—the components of your emotional system—that determine how you make use of those other sources. Let's review these components and see how they can be used to get you motivated and keep you motivated.

Become a Positive Thinker

The most important internal resource you have for motivating yourself is your thoughts. In the last chapter, we saw how destructive distorted thinking can be, and how useful constructive inner dialogues are. It's easy to see why negative thoughts such as *I'm a terrible writer, I'll never be able to get this report done—it's a dumb policy to have weekly reports* can only undermine your confidence and enthusiasm, whereas positive statements such as *I've done so many reports I should be able to knock this one right out—these weekly reports are a good way for me to see areas that need my attention* have the opposite effect. Positive thoughts are a tonic to your motivation; negative thoughts are a toxin.

There are a number of techniques you can practice to become a positive thinker: (1) using motivational statements, (2) playing mental games, (3) focusing your thoughts, (4) using mental imagery, (5) engaging in productive self-criticism, and (6) giving yourself meaningful goals.

Use Motivational Self-Statements. These are the statements that fortify your optimism, tenacity, and resiliency. They tell you that you have the capabilities and the drive to get a particular task done. Think of them as the statements you want to hear someone say to you in trying to bolster your confidence. But instead, you say them to yourself: *I can do this marketing plan. I've fully researched all the figures. No one understands the marketplace better. No matter what, I'll get the plan done.*

If making such statements feels a bit awkward to you, what you need to do is develop the habit of saying them. The following is an exercise to help you do that. You should practice it over the next thirty days, or as long as it takes for motivational self-statements to come easily to you.

■■■

Exercise for Learning to Make Motivational Self-Statements

1. Each morning as you first sit down at your desk, give yourself one motivational self-statement. Examples: "I can get done all that I have to do today"; "I am going to have a very productive day."

2. Each time you are given a new assignment, immediately give yourself a few motivational self-statements: "I can do whatever it takes to get this assignment done," or "I can stick with it until it is successfully accomplished."

3. Put your most powerful motivational self-statements on index cards: "I know what to do to start this task and finish it success-fully," "I've got what it takes to stick with it," "Nothing will get in the way of my getting this job done." Put the cards where you can readily see them, and read the statements to yourself when-ever you feel your motivation flagging.

■■■

Generally, you know when motivational self-statements are needed. The indications are negative thoughts (*I'll never get this marketing plan done*) and inertia (you sit staring at the walls because you feel overwhelmed by what you need to get done). Just start giving yourself motivational self-statements. By saying them over and over, you begin to believe them; that's the first step to getting back on track with the task at hand. In the next section, we look at another technique for mobilizing your thoughts to motivate you.

Play Mental Games. Two games I've found to be useful in helping motivation to kick in are Day One and Best Workday. Though different, they both involve using your emotions productively and are based on the same premise: mental fantasies can guide you to an optimistic train of thought, which not only keeps the negative thoughts at bay but starts up positive arousal, which, as we see later, motivates you to take action.

First, here's how you play Day One.

■■■

Exercise for Learning to Play Day One

1. Pretend this is the first day of a new job. Let's say the task that you are finding so difficult to begin and work on is a long letter to

a potential new client detailing all the benefits to be gained by choosing you over the competition. Although you've written dozens of these letters in the past, have what you can offer down pat, and have taken lengthy notes about what the client is looking for, you're still having a hard time sitting down and putting the two things together. Now, imagine that this is the first day of a new job. You've inherited this task from your predecessor, who gave you all the relevant information.

2. Approach the task as if this really *were* your first day on the job. Chances are, you would be fired with enthusiasm to just jump in and get going right away on whatever needed to be done. You would do that by starting off with one task—reviewing the list of the client's needs and prioritizing them, for example—and then moving on to others. By putting yourself in this different frame of mind— the task is new and fresh, not the usual drudgery, and hence it's exciting—you are able to approach it with eagerness and optimism.

3. Use Day One as a conditioned response. Recall from Chapter Two that the conditioned relaxation response is a way to reprogram your arousal by instantly and automatically summoning calming images at the first signs of arousal. Here, you reprogram for motivation by using signs saying "Day One" to instantly call up feelings of enthusiasm, confidence, and eagerness. Put up such a sign in your office, or set your computer to have "Day One" flash on the screen when you turn it on. Say *Day One* over and over in a forceful voice. Imagine the energy and enthusiasm you have on the first day of a new job. Eventually, you will be able to condition yourself to have energy and enthusiasm just by looking at those signs.

■■■

Exercise for Learning to Play Best Workday

1. Imagine this is the best day you've ever had in your working life. Imagine you are full of energy and ideas, you're getting lots of things accomplished, and people are responding to what you've done with much praise.

2. Imagine some of the specifics you might do on the best workday. Suppose one of the things is writing an innovative sales plan. You review sales figures, analyze trends, make charts and graphs, give explanations, put everything together, and present it to the staff, and they say how wonderful it is.

3. Get in touch with the optimism, enthusiasm, and confidence you would feel on such a day. Once you imagine yourself forging ahead on the specifics of one of the things you do on the best day, it becomes easy to tune in to the positive feelings you would experience then.

4. Use Best Workday as a conditioned response. (Follow the instructions under playing Day One.)

■■■

Focus Your Thoughts with Time Lock and Focal Lock. These two practices are another way that your thoughts can be directed to motivate you. They help you confront procrastination, avoidance, and inertia by setting aside time and space to redirect them.

We've all experienced days when we start out feeling fully motivated and energized, but by midmorning we realize we haven't gotten anything done. This starts a whole negative cycle of loss of confidence, enthusiasm, and tenacity. It seems impossible to get anything done, and then it becomes impossible to get anything done. Here's where you can use Time Lock.

Time Lock is a period of time that you block off for doing intense work. You tell your coworkers that you don't wish to be disturbed then, and you hold all your calls. In essence, you put a little bubble around yourself and designate the time and space for an area of intense work. The time can be ten minutes, half an hour, two hours. Don't make it longer than you think you can use, or you'll start feeling again as though you can't get anything done. Then, because you have announced that this is time for intense work and because others know about it, you must use it—wisely. And you will.

To facilitate use of that time, you can practice Focal Lock. This is a period during which you focus on allocating tasks to be done during Time Lock and then write them down. Using the example of the day that begins well, let's say that midmorning you find you're playing Solitaire on your computer and checking your mailbox three times (even though you aren't expecting anything important). Eventually you acknowledge that your motivation has disappeared. So you make a list of all the things you would like to do during your Time Lock period. Let's say you set aside an hour. You might designate it for five phone calls you need to make and two memos that must be written before the end of the day. This assures you of getting something done during Time Lock, but your accomplishments serve to reinforce your belief in your ability to do your job, and they inspire you to carry on doing more.

Sometimes it's helpful to set aside a Time Lock period at the beginning of the week. Make it for four hours, and use it to do all those tasks for which you lack motivation. Be sure to make your list of tasks before the designated period, so you can use the time most productively.

■■■

Emotional Intelligence at Work

I hate to do all the invoices connected with my work. I was very good at finding ways to avoid doing them. But I got so far behind that it was causing serious problems, like poor cash flow. I couldn't afford to have that happen.

Here's what I do now. Each week, usually on a Thursday afternoon, I tell my assistant that I am not to be disturbed for the next two hours. I then go into my office and only do the invoicing, nothing else.

Two hours later I feel great because I've gotten it done. In the old days, it would have taken me a week to get it done, not two hours. (Madeleine T., owner of catering business)

■■■

Use Mental Imagery. Humans have the unique ability to visualize themselves in almost any situation regardless of where they are or what they're doing at the time. We have already seen in the section on problem solving how visualizing the outcome of a particular situation can help you evaluate the route you take to get there. Here mental imagery is used to galvanize us into activity by visualizing ourselves doing the activity. We create the perception through our visualization that we can carry out a particular task, and before long, we find that we can.

Here's how mental imagery works. Imagining something often induces the physiological responses that actually doing the activity causes. If you imagine yourself running down the street to catch a bus, small but measurable contractions in your muscles occur, similar to those you have as you actually run. Visualizing yourself making a stellar presentation can trigger the same physiological arousal, namely enthusiasm and confidence, that actually making the presentation evokes. It then takes just a tiny effort to use that arousal in the real-world situation, to motivate you to work on the presentation.

The other aspect of mental imagery with regard to motivation is that it is based on imitation. You've seen how the most effective way to learn a new behavior is often to imitate someone else who does it successfully. A shy salesperson can watch his coworker begin a sales pitch and imitate him as a way to practice and learn how to do it. Similarly, use the mental image you have of yourself making that stellar presentation and imitate in reality what you see yourself doing in your mental imagery.

All of this means that by identifying, refining, and practicing in your mind the steps necessary for successfully staying on course (I like to think of this process as a mental rehearsal), you make it easier for yourself to be motivated to carry out the steps in real life. Here is an exercise to help you do so.

■■■

Exercise for Using Mental Imagery

1. Relax. Calm yourself by closing your eyes and taking deep breaths.

2. Call up in your mind the task for which you are feeling unmotivated. Let's say it's writing an employee evaluation. Vividly focus on the sensations you will experience in that situation. See yourself at your desk, feel the pages of the evaluation form under your fingers, and hear phones ringing and people talking in the corridor.

3. Imagine yourself struggling with the task. The form is in front of you. You start to write something and then you cross it out. You go to the next part of the evaluation and are unable to write anything. You feel frustrated; perhaps you pace around your office.

4. Imagine yourself regaining your composure. You sit back down at your desk, you feel calm and in control, and you begin writing out one section of the form.

5. Imagine yourself succeeding. See yourself working your way through the evaluation form, filling in each section with constructive criticism and suggestions for improvement.

6. Imagine yourself feeling good. You have finished the report, you are pleased that you got it done, and you're proud that you had such useful things to say.

The value of this exercise is that it enables you to see the previously perceived insurmountable task as being a manageable one. By looking at it step by step, and by talking yourself through the task from beginning to end in your mind, you see yourself as being successful—you accomplish the task. This then spurs you on to undertake the task in reality.

■■■

The mind is a very powerful organ, and our thoughts and imaginings can exert a tremendous influence over our behaviors in real life.

Use Productive Self-Criticism. There's no greater slayer of confidence and enthusiasm than negative criticism. Think of the example in Chapter Two of the boss calling an idea suggested in a meeting "harebrained." Conversely, there's no better way to help a person sustain momentum and optimism than by offering productive criticism: "That was a very useful report on ergonomic changes we could make in the office. You researched all areas of the issue very thoroughly. I felt the recommendation for buying all new chairs might be too expensive, but perhaps you could look into ways we might modify the chairs we already have."

You can see how the person who prepared the ergonomics report is going to be highly motivated not just to look into modifying the chairs but to write similar reports, tackling equally difficult tasks. Productive self-criticism works in the same way, except you're the person giving the productive criticism to yourself.

For most of us, productive self-criticism doesn't come easily, since we are too accustomed to seeing all the things we do as being wrong. But productive self-criticism is the key to self-motivation, and here's an exercise to learn how to use it.

■■■

Exercise for Using Productive Self-Criticism

1. Choose a task that you are having particular difficulty with at the moment. Let's say it's writing a report to your boss explaining why your department can't cut any employees in the new downsizing scheme.

2. Look at what you've done so far and tell yourself why the writing is good, effective, and helpful—and if it isn't, how you can improve it. Continuing with the downsizing example, you review the five points you've already written down and tell yourself they make sense: they're rational, and they clearly illustrate why productivity will go down if you cut even one employee. You also see that you are a little long-winded in some of your explanations, so

you suggest to yourself that you tighten up the writing a bit to make your points come across more strongly.

3. Feel good about what you've done. Recognize that you've done a good job, and you can fix what needs fixing. This acknowledgment gives you the confidence, optimism, and enthusiasm to carry on with the rest of the report.

What may have been keeping you from continuing with the report before you gave yourself productive self-criticism was negative self-criticism: "The points aren't convincing. The boss won't be able to make sense of what I've written." Just as we learned in Chapter Two that a good way to cut off destructive automatic thoughts is to learn to use constructive internal dialogues, the same is true here: you can avoid the demotivational effects of negative self-criticism by immediately giving yourself productive self-criticism.

■■■

Emotional Intelligence at Work

One of the things I noticed about myself early in my career as an architect is that I was very self-critical. After working on a project for a week, I would tell myself it was no good. I found a million things that were wrong with it. So I would give up and go on to another idea. The same thing would happen again. Of course I never finished anything. I began to get discouraged.

One day my boss took me aside and asked what the problem was. I told him I would start out just fine, and then I would look at my work and find fault with it and lose my motivation. He told me all architects find fault with their work. The key thing, he said, is after you find the faults, you tell yourself how to do it better.

I internalized his message. I would work on a project for a few days and then I would start to criticize it. But now I would respond to the criticisms. I would have a dialogue with myself and play both parts, giver and receiver of criticism. I would have each side listen to the other. It was sort of a Socratic dialogue with myself.

Now when I engage in this productive self-criticism dialogue, I
find I improve my work. I'm telling myself how it could be better, and
I find that very motivating. (Jennifer L., architect)

■■■

As you look at your project and tell yourself where it needs to
be improved, you give yourself direction, you tell yourself what you
need to be working on. This is what we look at next.

Give Yourself Meaningful Goals. When you are motivated, you have
a clear sense of direction; you know where you're going. When you
lose your sense of direction, your motivation tends to leave you.
Here's where goals come in.

A goal is a specific objective. It stimulates your arousal. Your goal
to become the top copywriter in your department stimulates your
desire to accomplish the goal. This arousal is then transformed into
energy that helps you to achieve your objective.

If you set up as a goal something that is too easily accomplished,
such as merely keeping your job as a copywriter, it becomes boring
and does not stimulate you. If, on the other hand, you make it too
unrealistic—you want to make a million dollars as a copywriter—
you run the risk of setting yourself up for disappointment and failure. The idea is to give yourself a goal that excites you, that keeps
you reaching, and that can conceivably be accomplished, albeit
with an extraordinary effort and some luck thrown in.

When your goal is extremely ambitious (becoming the best
copywriter in your company, even though there are many veterans
with years of awards behind them) you can sometimes get overwhelmed and lose your drive. This is where you need to constantly
reinforce your tenacity. Here are some tips for helping you do that.

■■■

Tips for Effectively Using Your Goals

1. Acknowledge your progress toward reaching your goal. Give
   yourself a dose of positive reinforcement to spur you along. In the

copywriter example, you might point out to yourself that after your first three projects you were moved on to one of the most important ones. On the next one, your manager singled you out for praise when that campaign had sales exceeding projections. You are still being given major assignments. By acknowledging your progress, you can see that you are indeed getting nearer your goal, and this recognition inspires you to continue working hard and moving ahead.

2. Focus on how close you are to your goal. In seeing how far we have to go, it's too easy to overlook how far we've come. Even if you're only 25 percent of the way toward meeting your goal, tell yourself you are one-fourth of the way there, not three-quarters of the way from meeting your objective. You can feel happy that you went from 0 percent to 25 rather than dejected that you still need to go from 25 to 100. In the copywriter illustration, let's say there are twenty people in the department and you are now fifth in importance, or one-quarter of the way to being number one. Tell yourself, "Wow: in three years I've worked my way up to number five in the department." This helps motivate you to keep on track to go the rest of the way.

■■■

In this section on becoming a positive thinker, we've seen how our thoughts can be mobilized to get our motivation going and keep it working. We've glimpsed how our arousal comes into play here, say, as a catalyst to keep us moving toward an objective. In the next section, we look more closely at how arousal is also a key to self-motivation.

Use Arousal to Generate Energy

In its purest and most primitive form, motivation is recognized by an increase in physiological arousal that incites or impels us. This is true whether you're a copywriter working hard to be the best in your department or a cat trying to capture a finch flitting about the garden. Motivation is intrinsic to humans and animals, and it is fueled by an increase in physical arousal, an expenditure of effort.

Even such seemingly sedentary and almost mindless activity as filling out invoices requires an expenditure of energy (your eyes and fingers are moving; your brain is figuring out the numbers). But without an increase in physical arousal, triggered perhaps by a desire to get the job done or by the imagined joy that will be experienced when the job is done, you have no energy to finish the invoices. You need to learn to arouse yourself, mobilize that arousal, and turn it into energy. You then mobilize the energy to help you accomplish your task. Here are some ways for you to use your arousal in motivating yourself.

Move Around. I'm sure you've had moments of low energy, where you just seem to be stagnating at your desk, unable to get anything done. You fight to keep your eyelids open and your head off your chest. Then you walk downstairs and across the length of the building to the mailroom. When you get back to your desk, you feel astonishingly refreshed and ready to get back to work. If you do aerobics, go running, or work out in a gym during lunchtime, you have no doubt noticed how energized and reinvigorated you are afterward.

There's a physiological explanation for all of this. When you exercise, your blood pumps faster so more nutrients can be brought to your muscles, organs, and other parts of the body (remember what happens during the fight-or-flight response), and your breathing increases so that more oxygen is delivered to your cells. When you return to your desk after the stroll to the mailroom or your workout in the gym, your body and brain have had the nutrients they need replenished (to a varying degree, of course, depending on the amount of exercise). This keeps you from feeling drowsy (the doziness was probably caused by insufficient oxygen) and helps your brain function better.

There's another explanation for why we feel so refreshed when we exercise: exercise stimulates the production of endorphins (recall the section on humor in the preceding chapter), and the release of endorphins causes us to feel good. So whenever you feel your motivation flagging or your energy lagging, get up and move around. Below are some tips for bringing movement into your workday without pumping iron at the gym or doing laps around the pool.

■■■

Tips for Moving Around in the Office

1. Walk whenever you have the opportunity. Use stairs instead of elevators. Use the restroom farthest from your workspace. Walk to the copyroom instead of having someone else take your work to be copied. Go talk with Ralph in Accounting when you need an excuse to get up and walk around.

2. Do some simple stretches. Take five minutes and do a few almost imperceptible exercises sitting at your desk. These can be neck stretches (rotate your head in a semicircle back and forth along your chest), leg lifts (lift one leg at a time until it's parallel to the floor, and hold a few seconds), arm stretches (raise one arm at a time over your head and reach to the opposite side). Please note: if you have back or other physical problems, check with your doctor first before doing any of these.

3. Get up from your desk at lunchtime. Many of us bring sandwiches and quickly eat our lunches while sitting at our desks. If this is what you normally do, walk out to the corner shop, the snack wagon, or your cafeteria to get something to drink. At the very least, walk to a far-off water cooler. If you're going to buy something to eat and bring it back to your desk, be sure to go out and get it yourself rather than have someone else get it for you. The time you spend doing this is well rewarded by the renewed motivation you feel from just a small expenditure of energy.

4. If your office is totally private, then you can do some more vigorous exercises, like jumping jacks or running in place.

■■■

Emotional Intelligence at Work

I'm in the advertising business and I have to do a lot of presentations to clients—show them the commercials I do. It's a pretty competitive business, and you only get one chance to pitch the client. I find it is very important to be enthusiastic during the pitch. The clients sense it, and it makes me feel good, too.

So what I do to get that pumped up feeling before the presentation is a few minutes of the Ali Shuffle. I move around, throw a few jabs, I'm on my toes, I do a few ducks, a few combos. Even before a round is over I'm hot. I'm ready for my client and feeling good. (Jeffrey C., advertising account manager)

■■■

Relax. It might seem paradoxical to tell you to *relax* in order to get your energy level up, after I've just suggested you do the opposite. But the truth is many of us are so exhausted from long workdays, active families, and other commitments that we are too tired to muster up the motivation we need to get our work done. Drowsiness, heaviness, and immobility may be caused by exhaustion as much as by lack of oxygen to the cells or nutrients to the organs. The manifestations are the same, but the cause is different.

If exhaustion is the cause of your inability to arouse yourself, then you need to set aside regular, extended periods to relax. You need this time to let those overactive cells, organs, and circulatory and respiratory systems—as well as your emotional system—rest, refuel, and regenerate. Think of how energized you feel when you come back from a relaxing vacation.

I recommend an hour a day, but if all you can manage is twenty minutes, then that is certainly better than nothing. Use this time to be solitary, quiet, and undisturbed. Take a bath, read a book, listen to music, meditate. Close your eyes and tune out all thoughts of work.

Obviously, these activities are to be done at home. There's a familiar way to get a little relaxation in the office (depending on how private your workspace is). It's called a catnap. Some people find that by putting their heads down on the desk and actually going to sleep for five or ten minutes they awake amazingly restored (note, though, that others find just the opposite). You may need some sort of timer to be sure you wake up when you want, or a call from your secretary or an understanding colleague. You certainly wouldn't want someone to come in and catch you asleep on the job.

We've discussed the importance of arousal in helping to motivate us. Now we look at how we can use our actions and behaviors toward the same end.

Utilize Productive Actions and Behaviors

You can be in a positive frame of mind to start and complete a particular job, you can be filled with energy to do what it takes to get the job done, but you might find something is still missing. You're still not motivated. What's missing is certain actions you can take, certain behaviors you can use to give yourself that final push.

In this section, we describe two ways you can utilize productive actions and behaviors. The first is to break down a task or assignment into minitasks. The second is to monitor your behaviors to see which ones are particularly effective in helping to motivate you.

Break Work down into Small Tasks. You often feel overwhelmed by assignments. There's too much to do, there's too little time in which to do it, and you don't have all the resources that will enable you to do it. Once you begin to feel overwhelmed, all sorts of negative feelings—frustration, anxiety, fear—begin to take over, and before you know it your motivation is out the door and you're unable to get anything accomplished.

Indeed, a thirty-page report is an awesome endeavor. But if you think of it as thirty one-page reports, or six five-page reports, it seems quite manageable. Take any project for which motivation is eluding you, and break it down into minitasks; then do each one. Here are some suggestions for doing so.

■■■

Tips for Breaking Work down into Small Tasks

1. Make a list of all the tasks related to the project at hand. For the thirty-page report, here are some of the tasks that might be involved:

    Get market research data from Marilyn.

    Get sales figures from Jonathan.

    Get figures on similar product launches.

    Ask Harold for copy of his last report.

    Make list of what I want the report to cover.

    Do an outline.

    Write Section 1.

    Write Section 2.

    Write Section 3. . . .

    Write Section 8.

    Write Conclusion.

    Each task is manageable. The writing is probably the most difficult task, but no section is more than four pages long. Although each task can still cause you a certain amount of anxiety, fear, or frustration, the amount is significantly less than that caused by thinking of the report as one major job. Consequently, it's easier to keep your confidence and enthusiasm at a level where they help sustain your motivation.

2. Make your first task a guaranteed success. In the case of this report, there's a certain sequence to be followed: you need to compile the research and documentation before you can do the outline, and you need to plan the outline before you can begin

writing any of the sections. So you can't just begin anywhere. It makes sense to gather the materials you need first, so start off with the easiest one. Jonathan already has the sales figures. But if he's almost impossible to get in touch with, then don't begin with him. If Harold is not very generous about sharing advice or expertise, then don't begin with him, either. If you know Marilyn to be very helpful, forthcoming, and available, then that's a good place to begin. The first success fuels your optimism, which gives you the motivation you need to undertake the next task.

■■■

As you move from task to task, even though some may be more problematic than others, you gain momentum, your confidence builds, and the thirty-page report is no longer an impossible and unrealistic undertaking but a feasible project, made up of small, manageable tasks. The project can be accomplished.

Monitor Your Behaviors. As we learned in Chapter Two, behavioral patterns are tendencies, or actions that we do over and over. By monitoring them and then examining how they affect your motivation, you can decide which ones to continue doing and which ones to discard.

Let's say these are actions you've taken in the past when preparing a long report:

- Get advice from lots of people.

- Study research until it's practically memorized.

- Write introduction before any of the other sections.

- Take lots of notes on index cards.

- Pace around office when writing comes slowly.

Make a chart to keep track of the effectiveness of each behavior. Note possible revised behaviors. Here are four examples of what such a chart might look like:

Behavior	Consequences	Effectiveness	Revised Behavior
Getting advice from lots of people.	It took a lot of time; I often didn't do what people suggested.	I spent too much time; I hated going around to everyone; so I put off doing it and then alienated people when I didn't follow their advice.	Be more selective in people I get advice from, choosing those with whom I seem to agree, and who won't be too offended if I don't follow their advice.

Behavior	Consequences	Effectiveness	Revised Behavior
Write introduction before any of the other sections.	I have to totally rewrite it at the end.	I procrastinate terribly on doing the introduction, because I know I'll just have to redo it.	Take notes on what I think might go in introduction, but save writing until the end.

Behavior	Consequences	Effectiveness	Revised Behavior
Taking lots of notes on index cards.	I'm left with a huge pile of cards to organize.	Once I've organized them, they charge me up because it makes it seem as though the writing will be a snap—I just follow the cards.	None.

Behavior	Consequences	Effectiveness	Revised Behavior
Pacing around office.	I don't get anything done during that time; it makes me feel more frustrated.	The anxiety demotivates me.	Discard altogether. Instead of pacing, use any of the motivational techniques, from moving around to using self-statements.

You can see that by making this chart you learn what motivates you and what doesn't. Then, by revising behaviors or discarding those that don't work, you find it easier to become motivated and stay that way. The increased motivation you gain at each step galvanizes you toward successfully accomplishing the whole task.

In this section we've seen how you, the center of your universe, are your chief motivator. But sometimes, as strong as your desire is and as good as your intentions are, you just can't muster up the motivation you need. Fortunately, there are other sources to draw upon. The first one is other people in your life.

Supportive Friends, Family, and Colleagues

In the preceding section you've learned some very effective techniques and activities you can use to generate and sustain motivation; but sometimes they are just not sufficient—you need outside help. This is particularly true when you experience a major setback. Nothing can be lonelier, more difficult, more demotivating than believing you must face the situation all by yourself, with no one to help boost your spirits and get you back on track.

In this section we look at how to develop mutually motivational relationships, how to draw out from those relationships the motivation you need, and how to reciprocate.

How to Develop Mutually Motivational Relationships

You can't choose your family members and usually can't choose your colleagues; you can generally though not always choose your friends. But you are completely free to choose, from among these three groups, whom you would like to be part of your motivational support team. You might want to ask some people because they always have good ideas for getting out of a rut. Others are desirable because they always make you feel good by being so encouraging. And still others should be on your support team because you see them often and they understand you well.

Fix in your mind—before a crisis of motivation occurs—the people you can call upon for the help you need. This keeps you from feeling isolated, from saying, "There's no one I can talk to, there's no one who will be there for me." Such negative thinking only serves to set you back further. We all experience crises of motivation: relatively minor events such as rejection of a plan you worked on for many weeks, or major events such as a job layoff. Being prepared, with help lines in place, not only helps you survive and surmount the setback but it keeps you from fearing setbacks quite so much.

In developing mutually motivational relationships, you need to determine what it is you want from others, or else you won't know whom you want on your team. You'll draw out the motivation you need so that the relationships work best for you. But you need to know how to reciprocate, because if you just take what you need then the relationship is not mutual and will probably not continue for long. Let's look at these considerations further.

What to Look For. The three basic characteristics of your motivational relationships are trust, suitability, and availability. Trust is the key, because when you ask for help you are vulnerable; you want to reveal your vulnerability only to someone you can trust with it, someone who is caring, does not take advantage of the situation, respects confidentiality, and has your best interests at heart. Furthermore, if you don't trust the person, then you won't feel comfortable expressing your thoughts and feelings, and you won't be able to get the help you need.

Suitability is also important, because if a person is incapable of responding to your needs, then he or she won't be able to help you. Your best friend might be a terrific person, and you may have lots of good talks and good times with her, but she may not be able to bolster your motivation because that's just not the kind of person she is.

You also need different things from your motivational relationships. Sometimes you just need someone who's a good listener, who can really hear what you're saying. Maybe he can only respond by saying, "This must be very hard for you," or something similar; but simply saying that suggests he understands you, cares about you, and is giving you the opportunity to express what is bothering you.

Sometimes what you need is someone to give you concrete suggestions for how to get from point A to point B. This might be a colleague who understands the business you're in and can see ways out of your predicament. Recall the plan you've worked on for weeks and which is rejected. This person might be able to look at the report and see how it can be improved, so that you can learn for the next time and thus be more willing to face a similar project.

Other times you might need someone very loving and understanding to lavish lots of praise on you: "You're so smart and so competent. You have so much experience. Even if this plan bombs, you'll be able to do great the next time."

Availability is a bottom-line concern in developing your relationships, because if people are never around they can't help you. Your brother, whom you adore and are very close to, may not be appropriate for a motivational relationship because he travels so much, and when he's in town either he's at his girlfriend's or he never answers the phone. He's not a good candidate.

Bear in mind that these relationships are not formally constituted entities. You don't need to ask Gillian, "How 'bout establishing a mutually motivational relationship?" Look at the relationships you already have; see whom you can draw upon when your motivation is seriously in need of bolstering. Make a mental note of whom you would call for what, and then think of these people as your safety net.

What to Ask For. When we face a crisis, we often lose our sense of perspective and our ability to solve problems. Friends, family, and colleagues who can step back and are not totally consumed by the crisis can often provide help in these two areas.

Crises make us feel dejected, and when we feel dejected, despite all our good practice with constructive internal dialogues and motivational self-statements, we often allow distorted thinking to take over. *I'm a failure. I'll never be able to get out of this. I'll never be given work again.* As we've learned, this kind of thinking only makes the situation worse. Other people can help you by giving you a sense of perspective.

To help *them* do that, you need to tell them exactly what's happened. Tell them what you think about the situation, and ask them what they think. Let's take the extreme example of job layoff. Your company was recently downsized, your department was eliminated, and you've been let go; you feel extremely dejected. You talk a lot with the members of your motivational team. They remind you how miserable you were in your job, and how this job elimination may really be a godsend. They point out that although your company failed, the industry is thriving and there are plenty of jobs with better companies. They tell you *you're* not a failure, the company is; they say your expertise actually helped keep the company afloat. After you hear from your friends and colleagues how they see the situation, then you can reappraise it.

Because crises engender such powerful emotions, we tend to feel that we are overreacting, that we're losing it. Again, you can get some perspective from others here. Tell them what you're feeling: "I'm so angry I just wish that the president of the company would have a heart attack. I'm so afraid of the future that I feel like I'll end up eating in soup kitchens." Use *I-feel* statements. Then ask your

friends, family, and colleagues how they would feel in a similar situation. Chances are they'd feel very much the same way; this
knowledge reassures you that you are not losing your mind. Also,
airing your feelings helps you get in touch with them, and that helps
you bring them to a manageable level.

Crises are often so all-consuming that we see only hopelessness,
the impossibility of ever finding our way out. Our problem-solving
skills vanish. Here again, your motivation-building colleagues can
be invaluable. Explain the dilemma fully. Tell them what solutions,
if any, you've thought of, and ask them for theirs. The simple fact
that they're helping you find solutions is motivating, but so are the
proposed solutions themselves because they help you perceive that
there are ways to overcome the obstacles. There *is* a way out of the
dilemma; you *can* succeed.

Although you want your group behind you, bolstering and helping you, let them know that you are fully prepared and desire to do
the same for them. It's time now to look closely at the reciprocity
in a mutually motivating relationship.

How to Reciprocate. Reciprocity is generally the basis of any solid
relationship. These are mutually motivational, supportive relationships. These people are part of a team. This means that you are
there for your fellow members as much as they are for you.

Reciprocity doesn't always have to be in-kind. You might get
advice but give back home-cooked dinners. What is important is
that neither person in the relationship feels used, exploited, or
manipulated.

Let's take the job layoff situation. Naturally, because you are
going through such an unsettling time, you are more on the receiving end right now than the giving end. But there are certain things
you can do to make the people who are helping you through the crisis feel as though you are also there for them. Ask them what's going
on in their lives, show concern, give support, and offer advice. Follow through on past conversations ("How did the meeting with the

new client go?"). Referring back to earlier conversations indicates that you listen and that you care.

Show your friends and colleagues that you don't maintain the relationship solely for the benefit of your motivation. Call them just to say hello, to find out how they are. Talk about the positive feelings you have for them—not just in the context of the motivational support they give you, though that should also be acknowledged.

As you and your friends, family, and colleagues draw upon one another for motivational support, the relationships become stronger, you understand how you can each help motivate the other, and you take another step toward handling your worklife with emotional intelligence.

■■■

Emotional Intelligence at Work

I was never really a top student, though I got good grades because I worked very hard and studied all the time. I was very grade-oriented so I could get into the schools I wanted. Right up to medical school; I got into the med school of my choice.

That's when the horror began. The coursework was tremendous. I couldn't keep up. I felt overwhelmed. I was feeling really depressed, and I was doubting myself. I was beginning to feel that while I still wanted to be a doctor, I might not have the abilities.

Funny thing, though, on class quizzes I was doing OK—low B's. Still, I was feeling like I couldn't do it, and I felt like giving up. I think I would have if it hadn't been for two people, my grandfather and my uncle.

My grandfather, Poppy, was a cardiologist. For years we had a deep and loving relationship. During those first few months I felt he was one of the few people I could share my feelings with. He listened and sympathized. But most of all, he was supportive. He told me I could succeed. He told me that med school was tough, and if this one was too tough, I could look for another school, and that would be fine. He reminded me that almost all first-year med students are overwhelmed. He told me that I would do fine, but it would take a lot of work. And he said that no matter how I did, he would be there with his safety net. You know, his support motivated me—it helped me run the course.

I also had an incredible uncle, George. He gave me a lot of confidence over the years. He drummed into me the message to believe in myself. He got me to focus on how I was actually performing rather than how I felt I was performing. He pointed out that I *could* do it—I *was* doing it. After a while, every time I started to feel overwhelmed and depressed, I would call up my Uncle George for a blast of motivation. It always helped. (Kim H., doctor)

■■■

Next we look at other individuals who can help motivate you. They're easily found, constantly available, and always willing to help. And you don't need to give them anything in return.

Emotional Mentors

If you can think of one person whom you would like to have in your worklife, an inspirational hero, this is the person to choose as your emotional mentor. This person serves you by being your motivational model, the individual you would ask, "What would you, my mentor, do in this situation? How would you feel in this situation?"

It makes absolutely no difference whether your emotional mentor is dead or alive, real or fictitious. It might be Nelson Mandela, Wonder Woman, many of Harrison Ford's film characters, Hillary Rodham Clinton, Stephen Hawking, Elizabeth I, Pip of *Great Expectations*, Michael Jordan, Marie Curie, Henry Ford, Sojourner Truth.

The bottom line in choosing this person is that he or she must motivate you. Maybe you imagine yourself being Pip and just picking yourself right up after each letdown and carrying on. Or you might ask yourself, "How would Hillary Clinton deal with a boss who denigrates her in a meeting?" Or "I am Elizabeth I, and I won't let the Spanish Armada or anything else stand in the way of getting this job done." Thinking of your emotional mentor bolsters your confidence, enthusiasm, tenacity, resiliency, and optimism. Here's how to get the most out of your emotional mentor.

■■■

Tips for Effectively Using Your Emotional Mentor

1. Choose as your mentor an individual who is extraordinarily motivating for you.

2. Choose a motivational moment in that person's life, and relive it often. It might be Stephen Hawking discovering his black hole theories. Or Marie Curie receiving her second Nobel Prize for her work with radium. Or Michael Jordan listening to the roar of the crowd. Or Wonder Woman successfully fighting off an adversary. When you tell the story of that moment to yourself, throw in as many details as possible so you can really feel the experience.

3. Call upon your mentor often. The more you call up your mentor and relive an inspirational moment in that person's life, the easier it will be for your mentor to evoke your feelings of motivation. Just imagine yourself feeling cloistered by your job, shut in by all you have to do, unable to work your way out of the morass. Then summon up the moment when Nelson Mandela was finally released from prison after twenty-eight years of incarceration, and imagine the exhilaration he must have felt as he walked down the streets of Johannesburg, a free man. You might think to yourself, *Nelson got through one day at a time, believing he would prevail. I'm going to get through one task at a time, and I will prevail.*

■■■

As with other conditioned responses, eventually you won't have to retell the motivational story; simply saying your mentor's name or fixing your mentor's image in your mind will spur on your motivation.

Next we turn to the fourth source of motivation, your environment, and what you can do make it more motivating.

Your Environment

Most of us don't have a lot of control over our work environment, but there are nevertheless a number of things that we can do to make our workspace more motivational. Sometimes what this really means is making it less demotivational. The three areas we look at are (1) making your workspace a healthy place, (2) surrounding yourself with motivationally inspiring objects, and (3) organizing your workspace so that it works for you rather than against you.

Make It as Healthy and Helpful as Possible

Just as your own health can exert a tremendous influence over your level of motivation (think of how much work you want to get done when you have a bad cold), so can your environment. When we say *environment* we're referring to the air, light, sounds, and objects that surround your workspace. For you to be optimally focused and productive, these four elements must be as conducive to your well-being as possible.

Breathe Clean Air. We often don't notice that the air we're breathing is clean and fresh, but we sure notice when it isn't. Think of entering a smoke-filled meeting room or the office of an employee who works very long hours, apparently forgets to bathe, and never lets in any outside air. Or the meeting that suddenly changes its tenor when people begin yawning and nodding off. Stale air, depleted of its oxygen, is often the cause, though sometimes it can be air that's too warm. (Other times, as we well know, it can be boring speakers.)

In large offices, proper ventilation systems are mandated by the Occupational Safety and Health Administration (OSHA). These systems help circulate and clean the air, as so many office buildings today are hermetically sealed. If you feel there might be a problem with the ventilation system where you work, then speak to your maintenance department. If you feel the air is still stale or unclean, you can buy yourself a desktop air purifier that removes air impurities.

Although many offices these days are smoke-free environments, some still are not. If you feel that smoke is detrimental to your motivation (to say nothing of your health), you might talk with your manager to see if some arrangement could be made for smoke-free work areas. Failing that, use a desktop air purifier.

If you are lucky enough to have windows, open them if coworkers don't mind, the weather allows, and the noise on the street is not a factor. There's nothing like an infusion of fresh air to revive you. Try to go outside during your breaks, or at the very least stand by the door and breathe in some fresh air.

Odors also have an effect on motivation. You've probably noticed that if you're in a room with a bad smell, it's almost impossible to concentrate on anything other than the bad smell. On the other hand, you may have recognized how pleasant fragrances can affect you positively. Peppermint and citrus fragrances, for example, have been shown in studies to increase your levels of energy and concentration. Depending on your work situation vis-à-vis neighbors, you could put a little bowl on your desk with dried peppermint leaves or dried lemon rind, or place some citrus or peppermint oil on a disk designed to sit atop a light bulb. If you are going to use air fresheners, be sure they are natural and not chemical, as many people today have allergies to chemical products such as air fresheners.

Tune in Helpful Sounds; Tune out Hindering Sounds. Sound is arousing. By choosing the right sounds and eliminating the wrong ones, you can increase your motivational energy. You may have experienced a very desultory day, when you just can't seem to get your energy going and consequently your output is zilch. Then you get in your car, turn on some music, and feel something like a shot of adrenaline. You could just rip your way through dozens of invoices or spec lists or reports! But because many of us work in open workspaces, we can't just turn on a tape at our desks. If this is your situation, and if your job involves a lot of repetitive work for which music would be a stimulant, you might ask your boss if you can wear headphones and listen to music. Of course, you need to demonstrate to your boss that you're as efficient as ever, if not more so.

If office neighbors are not a consideration, then experiment with playing music in your office that you know tends to get you to work—the kind you put on when you clean the house. (I find that upbeat oldies, like early Beach Boys or Dion and the Belmonts, work just great for me.)

A few things to keep in mind while choosing your music: elevator muzak is *not* what you want, as that music is meant to be calming and you want something stimulating. Also, certain kinds of classical music can have different effects. Mozart, for example, has been found in studies to increase mental acuity. Baroque music with fewer than sixty beats per minute can help promote concentration. Try different kinds of music to see what produces the best results for you.

Offices are filled with all kinds of sounds, many of which just become white noise while others can be real irritants and demotivators. Think of construction work on the floor below, or a coworker in the next cubicle who speaks on the phone constantly and very loudly. You might try earplugs, if you your job doesn't involve a lot of talking with other people. If your coworker is so distracting that you just can't learn to tune out, then you might ask your supervisor about moving your workspace. Sometimes it's just a question of acclimating yourself to new and irritating sounds. Try taking deep breaths to relax yourself. Practice the techniques you've learned for not getting angry or frustrated.

■■■

Emotional Intelligence at Work

Once a week my staff of six has to spend at least two hours doing paperwork that they dread. It's not difficult, just grunt work. On one paperwork day a staff member asked if anyone would mind if he turned on his portable tape deck. No one objected, and so the music started. I noticed that people seemed to enjoy it and, in fact, finished their work about twenty minutes ahead of time.

We now have a powerful stereo in the office, and I swear that playing music at different parts of the day creates a more enthusiastic and productive staff. (Jonette A., sales manager)

■■■

Use Light Advantageously. In 1982, Dr. Al Lewy of the University of Oregon and Norman Rosenthal of the National Institute of Mental Health conducted a series of studies that demonstrated how lighting can affect one's motivation. They examined a large number of people who became depressed during the winter months and concluded that their depression was due to a lack of ultraviolet (UV) rays hitting the brain's occipital lobe. Called SAD (seasonal affective disorder), this state of mind is easily cured by sitting under an ultraviolet light.

If you have windows, take advantage of natural light where you can. People often have a tendency to draw blinds or shutters because bright light can sometimes be blinding as it falls on desks. Then they forget to open the window coverings when the sun is no longer shining directly on them, thereby losing out on those motivating UV rays.

So where you have natural light, let it in at times when it doesn't blind you or make you drowsy. If you don't have natural light, you may want to install a UV bulb in your lamp; if you just have overhead lights, ask if you might have a UV bulb installed. Be sure to explain the reason why.

Color also has to do with light. We see different colors based on the varying length of the light rays hitting our retina. And colors also affect our motivation. Think of how much work you would want to get done if you were in a room with all-black walls. Certain colors affect us differently. Red, for example, elevates our heart rate and blood pressure, whereas blues and greens tend to calm us down. Even though we each respond in different ways to a particular color, often as a result of childhood associations, many people find that yellow promotes creativity and communication, green enhances concentration, and red energizes. Experiment and see what works best for you. Although you may not be able to paint the walls of your office any color you want, you can probably put up tapestries or posters with the colors that you want surrounding you.

Surround Yourself with Motivationally Supportive Objects. Just as a picture of your favorite food can get you to salivate, a picture of your emotional mentor or an inspirational phrase can arouse your motivational energies. Put up photos, magazine clippings, and inspirational sayings or phrases that motivate you. It may be a photo of your daughter winning the martial arts trophy; of you catching a twenty-foot marlin; or Martin Luther King, Jr., saying, "I have a dream"; your favorite politician victorious on election night; Harrison Ford as Indiana Jones; or whatever you can look at to feel even a little charge of motivation.

Another way to make your workspace motivationally supportive is to use visual cues and reminder notes. Those little yellow Post-it notes are just great for that: "Call Ellen at Hampton Pharmaceuticals." "Do outline for report." "Get visuals together for presentation." These help keep us focused on what we need to accomplish. It's better to take a particular task, such as writing the outline or compiling the visuals, rather than the whole job ("Write report," "Do presentation"), so that you can feel a sense of progress by being able to peel off the Post-its when you've done the job. Of course, as soon as you take down "Do outline for report," you have to put up another note: "Write part 1 of the report." But you won't be constantly depressed by seeing the same note up there for days.

Organize Your Workspace So It Works for You Rather Than Against You
You're trying to work on a project but are totally immobilized because you can't find any of the papers you need. Relevant phone

numbers are on bits of paper who-knows-where, and there's no free surface on which to work. The project doesn't get started until after papers are put in proper files, the desk is cleaned off, and the phone numbers are assembled in one list.

Enthusiasm for a task is quickly sapped if your workspace isn't organized for ease and accessibility. I once knew a sales rep who wouldn't follow up his legwork because he couldn't be bothered to search in his office for the information he needed to do so. I knew a secretary who never got her filing in on time—she didn't like having to go to another office to do it. Whatever you must do to organize your workspace to fuel your motivation rather than squelch it is well worth the time and effort.

So far in this chapter, we've looked at how to use four sources to motivate you: yourself; friends, family, and colleagues; emotional mentors; and your environment. In each section, we've seen examples of different setbacks, from rejection of a proposal to loss of a job. In the next section, we explore how to cope with and surmount setbacks.

How to Deal with Setbacks and Create Comebacks

We all experience a setback at some point in our careers. The emotionally intelligent person knows not only how to cope with a setback and move on but how to learn from it as well. In this section, we see how setbacks affect us and how to move through the stages from setback to comeback.

How Setbacks Affect Us

A setback is a veering off course, a checking of progress. Events that can cause a setback are a poor performance appraisal, cancellation of a project, denial of a promotion, and job termination. In each situation, you're going along seemingly just fine, following a particular course, and suddenly—sometimes shockingly—you are told, "You are not performing as you should be." "Your project will never fly." "The promotion has been given to another person." "Your department is being disbanded."

Momentum comes to a grinding halt. Motivation plummets. Self-esteem hits the floor. You probably feel every negative emotion there is: anger, depression, fear, anxiety, and more. Depending on the severity of the setback, you may find the experience affecting other areas of your life: family, friendships, and nonwork activities.

People respond to setbacks differently. One sales rep, after losing a major account, falls apart and can't stay on top of his other accounts. Another sales rep in the same situation gets back on the phone and finds two new accounts. One person, after loss of a job, starts drinking heavily, while another ends up changing careers altogether, finding one that is more fulfilling. What differentiates those who deal well with setbacks from those who don't is resiliency, the ability to bounce back. What makes one person more resilient than another is not a resiliency gene but the ability to process and use the emotions engendered by the setback experience productively.

The good news is you've already learned many of the tools and techniques for doing this, in the earlier chapters on self-awareness and managing emotions as well as in this one. I like to think of these tools and skills as being part of the Comeback Toolkit:

- Tuning in to your feelings and interpretations

- Using motivational self-statements and constructive internal dialogues

- Keeping your sense of humor

- Practicing relaxation

- Engaging in physical activity

- Using problem-solving techniques

- Drawing from your support team

- Reassessing your goals and setting new ones

Let's look at how you can use these tools as you go through the emotional process of working your way from setback to comeback.

Moving Through the Stages from Setback to Comeback

Usually a setback is experienced as a loss: you've lost your path, motivation, confidence, self-esteem, and enthusiasm. You may have lost something more concrete as well, like a promotion, a raise, the go-ahead for a project, or your job. Although the speed with which one works through a setback and how one does it are unique to the individual, the stages that each person goes through are common to all people. They are disbelief, anger, yearning to turn back time, depression, acceptance, hope, and positive activity. We look at these in greater detail below; for now, recognize that you need to experience and manage each stage, successfully moving through each one. Failure to do so keeps you stuck in a particular stage and therefore that much further from your comeback.

The process of working through the different stages is a highly fluid one. At times you may experience several stages at once, at others you may flip-flop between stages, and sometimes you might return to a stage already passed. There is no right way to go through these different stages; the only proscription is that you thoroughly work through each one.

As we look at the different stages, we learn how to tune in to them and which tools and skills we can use to successfully progress from one stage to the next.

Stage 1: Disbelief. Your pet project has been canceled. You say to yourself over and over, *This isn't really happening to me. I can't believe this*. Disbelief, the first stage of a setback, serves an important function: it acts as a buffer between the shock of learning that some crisis has occurred and the torrent of powerful emotions sure to accompany such knowledge. Essentially, disbelief gives you a useful breather by denying that the crisis has taken place. Denying it for a prolonged period, of course, can keep you from moving ahead, but short-term denial can be quite helpful.

You're probably also saying to yourself, *This is the end of my career here. I'll never get another project here, or a job anywhere else.*

Everyone will think I'm so stupid. These are examples of distorted thinking. As we've seen, distorted thinking increases the likelihood of your making incorrect assessments and appraisals, and it acts as a powerful demotivator. So when you experience a setback, it's important to use your self-awareness skill of making accurate appraisals. Doing so enables you to look at the setback realistically, which in turn helps keep your emotional system in tune with the reality of the situation.

The other self-awareness skill to use here is getting in touch with your feelings. Disbelief and denial are fine at first, but then you need to become aware of your feelings so you can learn from them and move on. Because of the intensity of negative emotions you're likely to experience during a setback, particularly during the first stages, it's often tempting to not want to confront them. But one of the tenets of emotional intelligence is that we need to be open to negative feelings as well as the positive ones.

The emotional intelligence skill you can use here is called "positive denial." Like disbelief, it allows you to delay confronting your situation. Let's take the example of your company being downsized, a number of people laid off (including your boss but not you), and your department folded into another. Your assessments might go something like this: "I'm going to have to work twice as hard as I did before because half the people who normally did stuff are gone. My new boss is going to give priority to his old staff, and it will be like starting anew here. I'm sure I won't last long." When these thoughts become too distressful, tell yourself, "I know I have to deal with this, but I will think about it later."

What you're doing is giving yourself time to regroup and manage your emotions. At the same time, you acknowledge that you still have to face the situation but just not at this very moment. Facing it in little manageable periods enables you to become comfortable thinking about it. Ultimately you increase your emotional intelligence because you develop and reinforce your ability to experience negative feelings without being overwhelmed by them.

Gently acknowledging the reality of the setback and the accompanying feelings, and then accurately assessing the situation, are the first productive steps on the way to coming back.

Stage 2: Anger. You've begun to come to grips with the reality of the situation, but you're starting to say things like, "It's so unfair. They've made a huge mistake. I hate how they do things around here." This is the beginning of an anger feedback loop that feeds on itself and makes you feel much worse. You complain, feel bitter, and often push others away precisely when you need their support.

What you want to do first is use all the techniques you learned in Chapter Two for managing your emotions. These include everything from having constructive internal dialogues to relaxing. To prevent emotional outbursts and dissipate your arousal level, you might engage in some physical activity. You can also write a mock letter to the president of the company, telling her that you think her reorganization is the worst idea you've ever heard. (Don't send it, of course.)

Then, because anger is a cue that something is wrong, you need to look at the situation and see how it is wrong and where you want to go from there. In the process, you probably reassess your goals and priorities, and this helps you get back on course or seek another direction.

In the case of your department being merged with another, you might see that what's wrong is that this new work arrangement is not to your liking. However, you are still with a number of people you have worked with for several years and whom you respect, and you have heard that the departmental manager is a pretty reasonable person. Formerly, your goal was to continue being promoted in your department. But that isn't possible now, because there are too many others on the ladder. A few years ago, you were thinking about moving to another area of the company entirely, and you might still explore that possibility now. Anger helps you see what is wrong with the situation, what you can tolerate and accept and what you can't, and what might be a new direction.

Stage 3: Yearning to Turn Back Time. In spite of reassessment, you still wish things were as they had been. If only the stupid president hadn't made her stupid decision to merge the two departments, you would be happy as a clam back with your old boss and your old office. Yearning to turn back time is a bit like the disbelief stage in that it serves as a buffer protecting you from going head-to-head with the distressful experience. This nostalgia for the good old days before the setback helps you feel good, because you are reliving that time. But if you stay stuck in that mode for too long, you revert to the last stage and become very angry that those days are now gone.

The effective way of dealing with this stage is to recognize that you would indeed like to return to the times before the big change, but that's not possible. Then ask yourself, "So what do I do now? How do I get back on a forward-moving track?" The answer is that you have to take some productive action. It might be to look into that other department you were considering joining. It might be to talk with the new department manager and find out what changes she plans to make, and how you might be able to fit in. The key here is to begin to explore some realistic and practical actions you can take.

Stage 4: Depression. It can seem overwhelming to realize that you have to take productive action while you are feeling bad about yourself and shaky about making any decisions. How can you possibly muster the effort and the confidence to talk with the new boss, or learn about the other department? Just thinking about it is enough to send you to bed with the covers pulled over your head. That's precisely what many people do when they are depressed. Others find it hard to sleep, so they're exhausted during the day. Many shun friends, wishing to suffer alone.

This stage is the biggest hurdle on the road to comeback because depressing feelings and thoughts combine to create a sense of apathy and despair. You feel completely enervated and incapable of doing anything. But the encouraging thing about this stage is that it's a turning point, and once you've passed it, you are well on your way to coming back.

Here again, your techniques for successfully coming through this stage are familiar ones. Call upon your motivationally supportive friends, family, and colleagues for encouragement, advice, and help with problem solving. Use motivational self-statements. Surround yourself with people who are optimistic, and avoid being around people who are feeling low—some of the other members of your department, for example. Write in your feeling journal, because it's very important to be fully aware of your depressed feelings. As we've already learned, being aware of your feelings helps you manage them.

As you go through this stage, you acknowledge that you have had a setback and that you have suffered a loss. You no longer deny it with disbelief or yearning to turn back the clock. You have experienced it, you have resolved to take positive actions, and you are ready to move on.

Stage 5: Acceptance. As you enter this stage, your confidence is beginning to return because you know that you have weathered the worst of the situation. Your anger and depression are, for the most part, behind you (remember that you may revert to earlier stages or flip-flop from one to another), and motivation is beginning to return. You accept that your old work situation no longer exists, and that you are facing a new one.

In this stage you need to focus on your goals and desires and plan a strategy to realize them. Use your high self-awareness to get in touch with your desires. If you still wish to continue rising in the company but there is no hope of that in the merged department, then your goal might be to find a position in the other department you are considering. Manage your newfound enthusiasm by keeping it directed toward your goal.

Stage 6: Hope. Optimism returns. You have a meaningful goal in mind, you know the steps that will take you there, and you are both hopeful and reasonably confident of getting there. Your hope gives you sufficient arousal to get you to the next stage.

Stage 7: Positive Activity. You are finally taking actions that bring you back on track. You feel energized, encouraged, and ready to do whatever it takes to follow your new course. In a word, your motivation is nearly back. You've set up an appointment with the head of the other department, you've spoken with their people to find out what working there is like, and you've sought advice from your motivational team. To ensure that you hold on to your motivation, break down tasks into minitasks, monitor your behavior from time to time, and use your problem-solving skills to generate new and effective responses to any difficulties you might encounter.

Although these seven stages may not be relevant to anything you have experienced or are currently undergoing, it is very helpful to know in advance that there are predictable stages one passes through to move from setback to comeback, that there are skills—all of which you have already learned—for helping you get through each one, and that by using them you can generally work your way successfully thorough any setback. This knowledge alone can be motivating.

■■■

Emotional Intelligence at Work

The biggest setback I ever had was when I had spent more than six months coordinating a project of international scope and then the project was turned over to someone else. This was a devastating blow.

It seemed that the president of the company felt that I was not equipped to handle a project of such magnitude that would span three continents. The hell I couldn't! I had put the project together from scratch.

When I got the news I was dumbfounded. I remember sitting in my office in disbelief. Up until then I was a rocket. I had just turned thirty and I was moving up. Now everything seemed to come to a halt.

The next few weeks were really bad. I felt embarrassed and that I had instantly become a failure. I wasn't very productive, I didn't socialize with anyone. One day I was standing next to my secretary in the mailroom. She told me she was sorry about the project but she was sure there would be others. I began to share my feelings with her and she was very supportive. She pointed out that even though I was disappointed it was still great that I got the project started and I would get credit for that.

A few days later a good friend from the advertising department called to find out what had happened. I explained I had been told that the president thought I was too young to handle the job, that the people overseas who were much older would feel uncomfortable with me. I told him I thought it was political because the person who got the job wasn't much older than me. "Maybe so, but you might as well make the best of it," my friend said.

That advice rang with truth. Even if it was a case of politics, my best bet was to move on, create some successes, not wallow in my pity. I realized I had a lot going for me, I knew how to be successful, yet I had stopped being successful.

The next few days I started feeling better. I formed some new goals, got some things in the works. I ran some of the ideas past my secretary and my friend in advertising. They were encouraging and very motivating and both gave me good ideas to think about.

A few weeks later I got the green light on a very big project. And even if I don't go to conclusion on it, I know I will come up with other ideas. (Charlene D., marketing employee in a publishing company)

■■■

Putting All the Self-Motivation Skills Together

In this chapter, we've looked at setbacks primarily in the context of major crises: a canceled project, job loss. But as we've also seen, any demotivational activity or situation can cause a setback because it takes you off course, even if briefly. It can be a room with stale air, feeling incapable of getting the invoices done, being reprimanded by your boss, facing an overwhelming project, or working too hard.

What is so curious about setbacks is that they undermine motivation, yet it is precisely motivation that is needed to overcome the setback! This is not an insoluble conundrum, because what you've learned in this chapter is how to motivate yourself. So after being hit with a setback and suffering a period of demotivation, you review and put into practice everything you've learned about motivating yourself. This includes getting your thoughts, behaviors, and actions mobilized to bolster or restore your confidence and enthusiasm; seeking help with perception adjustment and problem solving from motivationally supportive friends, family, and colleagues; calling on your emotional mentor when you need a shot of inspiration and optimism; making your work environment as conducive to productivity and tenacity as possible; and, in severe situations, working through the seven stages from setback to comeback to reclaim your resiliency.

Becoming adept at motivating yourself, developing high self-awareness, and learning to manage your emotions are the three ways we've explored to help you increase and apply your emotional intelligence. Because the focus of this book is on using your emotional intelligence in the workplace, in Part Two we examine how your emotional intelligence can be put to work, helping you achieve the best possible relations with your coworkers, supervisors, clients, colleagues, vendors, and anyone else you may deal with during your workday.

Part Two
Using Your Emotional Intelligence in Your Relations with Others

Think of how much your workday involves interactions with other people. It might be your colleague in the next cubicle, people in the mailroom, your boss, members of your workgroup, clients, customers, or vendors. These interactions may involve negotiations (to have a package go out in the overnight delivery even though you missed the deadline, or to get your boss to approve your attending a conference), selling (your work group on a proposal, your client on your abilities), managing (your team, your subordinates), leading (colleagues working on your project, your clients), conflict resolution (with a vendor, with members of your workgroup), and team building (among your team, with your clients).

The key to making these relationships and interactions successful so that they benefit all concerned—not the least, you—is emotional intelligence. How you put your emotional intelligence to work is by recognizing and responding to the emotions and feelings of others, guiding those emotions toward productive resolution of a situation, and using those emotions to help others help themselves. Clearly your ability to do all of this enhances your position in your company. Not only do you get more done because you find consensus and cooperation, but others perceive you as being an indispensable person to have on their team, in whatever capacity.

In Part One, you learned how to increase your emotional intelligence on the intrapersonal level: by developing high self-awareness, becoming adept at managing your emotions, and learning how to motivate yourself. Now we put all these skills to work in pursuit of effective interpersonal relations on the job. We look at how you can develop communication skills, interpersonal expertise, and mentoring abilities. Finally, we see how a company whose employees learn to relate well to one another becomes an emotionally intelligent organization.

4

Developing Effective Communication Skills

The basis of any relationship is communication. Without communication—be it sign language, body language, e-mail, or face-to-face conversation—there is no connection and hence no relationship. The importance of effective communication skills to your emotional intelligence is crucial, and its value in the workplace is incalculable. Think of trying to resolve a conflict between two employees, or explain to your boss how his anger affects you, without being able to communicate well. In the first instance, you might further inflame one of the employees by hearing only the other person's side. In the second example, you could conceivably end up with a dismissal notice if your comments to your boss are taken as arrogance and insubordination.

In this chapter, we introduce the skills that enable you to communicate effectively and productively so that you can be assured that exchanges like these have the greatest chance for positive outcomes. These are the skills we explore:

- Self-disclosure: clearly telling the other person what you think, feel, and want

- Assertiveness: standing up for your opinions, ideas, beliefs, and needs while respecting those of others

- Dynamic listening: hearing what the other person is *really* saying

- Criticism: constructively sharing your ideas and feelings about another person's ideas and actions

- Team communication: communicating in a group situation

What imbues each of these skills and helps ensure their effectiveness is sensitivity. So before we discuss the skills in depth, we need to look first at the key role sensitivity plays in effective communication.

Using Sensitivity

In the first chapter, you saw that to increase your emotional intelligence you need to develop high self-awareness. This means examining how you make appraisals, tuning in to your senses, getting in touch with your feelings, learning what your intentions are, and paying attention to your actions. Many of the techniques that you've learned for doing so are the ones you apply here, too, the difference being that you turn your awareness outward toward the other person. You are becoming sensitive to the other person; sensitivity is another tenet of emotional intelligence. When you use your emotional intelligence in communicating with other people, you pay careful attention to how your communication has an impact on their feelings, thoughts, and behaviors, and you adjust your communication accordingly. Your sensitivity becomes a skill.

Suppose you have learned through experience that your boss has a rather inflated ego, yet you need to talk with him about his outburst in the meeting during which he castigated your proposal as a "harebrained idea." You certainly don't want to point out any character flaws in your boss or imply that they might have led to the outburst, because that would probably assault his ego. Your awareness of his behavior first of all leads you to recognize the size of his ego.

So you could begin the conversation by addressing his sense of himself: "Richard, I have always been so impressed by how even-tempered and rational you remain in meetings." Then you can slowly approach the problem you were having: "I don't know if you were aware of it or not, but in the meeting yesterday you seemed very angry when you said my idea was harebrained. Was it something I said that made you angry? I felt just terrible because I thought I had done something wrong."

Using sensitivity here leads you to check in after each sentence and see how Richard is taking it. Does he appear to be getting hot under the collar? If so, you might pull back a little, even asking, "Is this not a good time to talk about this?" That way you show you're sensitive to what Richard is feeling. By allowing him to feel safe talking with you and to know that you are aware of his feelings and how to protect them, you make possible a much more meaningful exchange.

One way you can learn sensitivity is by asking yourself, "How would I respond in that situation? What would be the best way for me to be told that?" In this case, you might ask yourself, "How would I like to be told about an outburst in a meeting? What's the least hurtful way a person could tell me about it?" Your answers should help you in forming your own strategy for using sensitivity when confronting a delicate situation. This is an example of using the building blocks of your emotional intelligence: you use emotion to facilitate thought. Another way you can learn sensitivity, although more problematic, is by trial and error. If you say to Richard, "Your outburst was uncalled for and insulting," and he yells back at you, "*Your* comment is uncalled for and insulting," you would presumably recognize that you are not as sensitive as you need to be and learn from that experience.

As we look at each of the five interpersonal communication skills, we see how your sensitivity to another person's feelings can be used to make the interaction with that person as successful as possible.

Self-Disclosure

Communication involves a back-and-forth exchange, a give-and-take. You are trying to understand the other person, the other person is trying to understand you, and you're each trying to get a message across. Sometimes the best way to get the process underway is to clearly express what you're thinking, feeling, and believing. *Self-disclosure* is the term we use for doing that. Not surprisingly, self-disclosure statements usually begin with *I think, I feel*, or *I believe*: "I think this proposal has merit." "I feel confused about the response it's getting." "I believe the best way to approach the others about it is with a preliminary memo."

Sharing your thoughts, ideas, and feelings in the workplace can sometimes be a scary experience. We're afraid that an idea might be disparaged, a thought might reveal our lack of knowledge, a feeling might suggest a weakness in character. There is no doubt that self-disclosure involves a certain amount of risk. I'm not recommending blanket self-disclosure, but rather strategic self-disclosure: you carefully choose what you care to reveal and when and how to reveal it; and you take into account both the nature of your relationship with the person to whom you are self-disclosing and the importance of the information you are sharing. By doing so, as you will see, you minimize the risks and maximize the benefits.

In the following sections, we describe six ways to use self-disclosure statements and feel comfortable in doing so: (1) acknowledge ownership of your statements, (2) make sense statements, (3) use interpretive statements, (4) make feeling statements, (5) use intention statements, and (6) make action statements.

Acknowledge Ownership of Your Statements

The key to use of self-disclosure is recognizing that certain experiences lead you to your thoughts, ideas, and feelings, and therefore they are *yours*, and yours alone. With this understanding, you not only validate your thoughts, ideas, and feelings by acknowledging that they are based on something concrete and personal—your own experiences—but you also accept that other people have their own thoughts, ideas, and feelings, based on their own experiences and therefore valid for them.

Suppose you're in a meeting to discuss productivity and you say, "It would be good for the department if we got some new computers." It's unclear whether you mean, "I think productivity in the department would be enhanced if we got new computers," or "I feel I would be able to work so much better if I had a faster machine," or something else altogether. It also suggests to others that you have no real position on the subject and no basis for making your statement. The latter explanatory statements, on the other hand, clearly reveal first how you think productivity can be enhanced or second how you could be more productive. They leave no room for confusion as to your position, and they suggest that your statements are based on prior knowledge or experience. At the same time, they leave the door open for others to express their thoughts and ideas on the subject, as your original statement does not.

Let's say you make the statement another way: "Everybody feels that productivity is down because we have such slow computers." Here you probably raise your coworkers' hackles by both dismissing the possibility that anyone might disagree and by denying everyone the opportunity of expressing their own thoughts. Furthermore, you call into question your credibility: how do you know what everyone believes? What do you base your statement on?

When you accept ownership of your statements, you are in essence telling yourself they have validity. This allows you to make your statements with confidence, coming from a position of strength. You become more adept at acknowledging ownership of your self-disclosure statements as you learn different ways of making them. The point to keep in mind as you learn each one is that it's fine to make the statements, since they're true for you; but be sure to listen to what others have to say.

Make Sense Statements

In Chapter One, we learned how our senses—seeing, hearing, smelling, tasting, and touching—are the sources of all our data about the world. Let's learn to use the data they give us to document the self-disclosure statements we make. This way the other person can experience the situation from our perspective and thus understand how we came to make our statement.

Suppose you say to your boss, "I didn't think you were too happy with my presentation." Let's say your boss *was* happy with it. She needs to know what you saw and heard that led you to that interpretation. You might say, "Well, when I was making the presentation you didn't ask any questions, you had a smirk on your face, and I saw you looking at your watch several times." But your boss says, "I was quiet because I thought you were doing such a good job, and you answered all the questions I might have asked. I was really happy you were so well prepared, and I was probably smiling. I kept looking at my watch because my daughter was sick and I had to call the doctor by two."

By using your sense statements to show your boss how you reached your conclusion, you enable her to clear up the misunderstanding. If she simply responds to your comment about her feelings about your presentation by saying, "Yes, I was very pleased," you probably still would feel unsure, and you wouldn't have a clue how you could have interpreted her responses so incorrectly. She also would be mystified as to how she could be perceived so incorrectly. So not only does your sense statement help clear up any misunderstanding about a particular situation, but it also helps you reach better understanding in the future.

By using your senses to document statements, you also help foil arguments because you make clear that you are not speaking from some absolute position of truth but merely recording and interpreting your data. The emotionally intelligent way of using sense statements is not to prove a point or prove you are right—because, recall, emotional intelligence acknowledges the right of others to their interpretations—but to explain how you arrived at your interpretation. Doing so opens the door for the other person to clarify any misperceptions.

Use Interpretive Statements

Interpretive statements reveal what you think or believe at a given moment: "I think it's time to go." "I didn't think you would be interested." "I believe you did this on purpose." They imply that you took certain information into account before making the statement: "It's three o'clock and we have another appointment at four." "In the past, you never showed any interest in seeing my weekly plans." "You told the client I had four other cases, which could only have led to their believing I couldn't handle this one."

But suppose new information comes to light: "The meeting has been moved to five." "I didn't know you always reviewed Peter's plans." "I wasn't aware you had told the client I'm the best at working with several clients at a time." Most likely you would revise your interpretations: "I guess we don't need to leave right now." "I can certainly understand how you would be interested in seeing my weekly plans." "I now see that you were trying to improve my relationship with the client."

By making interpretive statements ("I didn't think you would be interested"), you suggest that your interpretation is subject to revision, and thus the person listening to it does not feel boxed in by your certainty. Think of how your boss might respond if instead you say, "You're not interested in seeing my weekly plans." You might get into a bit of "Yes I am" "No you're not," which would take the communication nowhere and leave each of you feeling frustrated.

As in the case with sense statements, the more information you supply, the better the other person can see how you reached your interpretation and help you revise it, if necessary. You can document your interpretive statements with sense statements: "I've never seen you looking at anyone else's weekly plans." "I heard you telling the client I have four other projects I'm working on right now." Be open to and gracious about receiving new information: "I guess I didn't hear the whole conversation you were having with the client. Your telling them about how easily I manage the four other clients probably reassured them tremendously."

Make Feeling Statements

As we learned in Chapter One, it's important to get in touch with your feelings because they alert you to your comfort level in a particular situation and help you understand your reactions. They work in much the same way when you disclose them to other people: your feelings reveal information about your comfort level and the reasons behind your reactions. This then gives the other person a better picture of the situation and suggests ways it may need to be changed.

Suppose your boss has cut a week off your production schedule. You are working many hours overtime, you're scarcely seeing your family, and you're getting little sleep. You say to him, "I am really feeling overwhelmed by all the extra hours I need to work." (This is a clear *I-feel* statement.) "All last week I didn't get home until ten at night, and I worked on the weekend." (This is good documentation.) "I feel sad that I see my children so little and frustrated that we might not be able to meet the deadline." (These are precise feeling statements.)

It's easy to see how much useful information is conveyed to the boss. You show him how difficult the extra work is for you, which allows him to see why you have been a bit short-tempered and impatient with some of your coworkers, and why he caught you nodding off in a meeting. He may not be able to change the situation, but at least he can understand how it is affecting you and, hopefully, be sympathetic.

Most of us have probably been advised to keep our emotions at home, along with the bedroom slippers, because they don't belong in an office situation, where they can only cause problems. Indeed, in the above example, your boss might say, "Well, Marie, if you can't take it, then perhaps you should look for another job." Now, if your boss is an emotionally intelligent person—the kind of boss we all want to have—then he would recognize that you are facing an extreme situation, you've come to him to share your concerns and see if there's any way to find some relief, and he should take your disclosure seriously. But, as we all know, not all bosses have developed their emotional intelligence. Also, of course, there is some risk to disclosing your feelings, especially if done inappropriately, as you'll see in the following example.

Suppose instead of approaching your boss as you did, you burst into his office and say, "I am furious that we have to cut the production schedule by a week. It's so unfair. What do you expect us to do?" Your boss, no matter how enlightened, feels challenged, berated, and assaulted. He probably sees you as being overly emotional, incapable of handling stress, and a difficult person to work with. And he probably becomes angry, an emotion not conducive to a successful resolution of the situation.

The difference between the two examples is that the first one was handled in an emotionally intelligent manner, and the second one wasn't. To disclose feeling statements in an emotionally intelligent way, you need to tune in to your feelings, convey them accurately, and be sensitive to the respondent.

Tune in to Your Feelings

Before you can share your feelings with another person, you need to know what they are. In Chapter One, we discussed how difficult this is because we often disguise our emotions (it seems as though you're furious with your boss, but really you're feeling overwhelmed and frustrated) or we hide from them (you pretend that the situation is just fine and you can handle the extra work, but then you become irritable with your coworkers). I refer you back to the first chapter for reminders of how to get in touch with your feelings (for example, take into account any bodily changes and behavioral actions).

Accurately Convey Your Feelings

Even after tuning in to your feelings, it can be difficult to disclose them. Fear of repercussion is one reason; discomfort with any accompanying vulnerability is another, as is unfamiliarity with the process. The fear and vulnerability can be diminished by knowing that you use sensitivity (which we discuss below), thereby mitigating any negative repercussions. As for how to accurately convey your feelings, you begin by knowing what they are. Then you make a list of your feelings, using *I-feel* statements:

> "I feel overwhelmed by the amount of overtime I have had to put in."

> "I feel sad that I don't see my children anymore."

> "I feel depressed because I just can't seem to get on top of my work."

> "I feel fearful that we won't be able to make the deadline."

> "I feel frustrated that everything seems to be taking so much time to do."

Now, you probably don't want to share all of these feelings with your boss, because you don't want to reveal everything about yourself. Also, if you disclose the whole list he might not be able to grasp anything, and he might see you as a complainer. So you select those feeling statements that clearly convey to him what you're feeling so he can understand how you're responding to the situation and perhaps see how it might be ameliorated.

"I feel overwhelmed by the amount of overtime I have to put in" is a good one to begin with. Overtime is hours above and beyond the usual, so it is understandable that you might feel overwhelmed. Feeling sad that you don't see your children is another good one to disclose, because it conveys to him how your outside life is being affected. Feeling depressed is not a good one because it suggests you can't handle stress. Feeling fearful about the deadline is reasonable, but perhaps it's better conveyed by using *frustrated*, from the last example, which is not a good statement to use because you don't want him to know that everything is taking so much time to do.

People often confuse *I-think* statements with *I-feel* statements. You may hear them say, "I feel there's just too much work to do." "I feel it's not right that the schedule was cut back." "I feel we should at least have the weekends off." You can't feel there's too much work to do; you can feel exasperated, overwrought, or dispirited by all the work. Nor can you feel "it's not right"—but you can feel discontented, dismayed, or disheartened. If you can substitute an *I-think* or *I-believe* statement for your *I-feel* statement ("I believe we should at least have the weekend off"), then you're conveying a thought or a belief—but not a feeling.

Similarly, people often confuse a state of being with a feeling: "I feel exploited" is an example. Exploited is not an emotion but a state of being: you *are* being exploited. If you can insert *as though I have been* between the word *feel* and the verb participle *exploited*, then you are describing a state of being and not an emotion. This is not a question of semantics: feelings affect us in very different ways from thoughts or interpretations about a state of being.

One point you need to keep in mind is that you can convey feelings in ways other than just by verbally expressing them—in ways you may not even notice. Suppose your boss comes into your office and asks you to do a few new tasks. Your shoulders sink, your body slouches, your mouth turns down, you look at the floor. What you are conveying is that you feel dejected and disheartened. Or you respond by putting your hands on your hips and looking him straight in the eyes. You are conveying defiance: "I'm not going to do another thing!" Note that in each case you might actually *say* to him "OK." If you find your words (OK) conflict with your feelings (dejection), it's a sign to pay attention to your body language, to read what it is telling the other person. OK might be the appropriate response in this situation. But on the other hand, you may want to disclose your feelings about your boss's request: "I'm already feeling overwhelmed and frustrated by all the work I have to do. Is there any other person you could possibly ask to do those things?"

Be Sensitive to the Respondent

Emotions can be quite powerful. Think how anger can sometimes take over your whole body, so that it feels as though a freight train is going through. We often experience our emotions intensely, as do those people with whom we are sharing them. You don't want your emotions to overpower the other person, so you need to use sensitivity to detect how she is responding.

Suppose you begin to tell your boss how you're feeling about all the extra work, and he rolls his eyes and looks exasperated, as if to say, "I've heard enough of this. I don't want to hear it anymore." It may be that other people come to him telling him what a hard time they're having, and being powerless to change the situation he feels frustrated and exasperated. The message is that this is not a good time to discuss what you're feeling. So you should stop, perhaps saying something like, "This doesn't seem to be such a good time to discuss this." If a person is not in the right frame of mind to listen to something, he is not receptive. Gear what you say toward how the person seems to be reacting. If you sense the person is beginning to get angry or hurt, then it's usually a good idea to change what you are saying so that it is less hurtful and anger-producing, or curtail the discussion entirely for the time being.

You also need to choose both a time and a place that are appropriate. Catching a coworker in the corridor and saying, "I'm really angry that every time you use my computer you shut it off without closing down the applications" is not an appropriate place. It's public, a place where you ordinarily pass by one another, so it is not conducive to a meaningful discussion. Instead, ask your coworker if you might get together with her for a few minutes in her office or yours, or in the cafeteria if it can be private enough. In the same way, if you know ahead of time that your boss is having a very bad day, feeling extremely pressured about the deadline, then that is not an appropriate time to discuss your feelings with him.

It's also important to apply the appropriateness standard to what feelings you choose to disclose so that you are protected from possible unpleasant repercussions. As I mentioned above, it is not usually appropriate to tell your boss you are depressed. Depending on the circumstances, it could be appropriate with a coworker. It is often not appropriate to express anger; it can scare people. It's often better to say, "I'm very upset." Save *angry* for extreme situations, when you really need to convey the message.

At the beginning of the discussion of feelings, I said it's often useful to disclose them because it gives important information to the person listening. A key point to keep in mind is that you can't expect the other person to change or make changes as a consequence of your disclosure. Even after you tell your coworker how hurt you feel that she hasn't asked you to work on the new project, after she has been discussing it with you for days, you can't expect her to apologize, enlist you in the project, or include you in other projects. She may do so, but you can't have any expectations. All you can do is be sure that you get in touch with your feelings, disclose them accurately, and use sensitivity.

Use Intention Statements

By revealing your intentions, you let the other person know what your desires are. When the two of you are clear about what you want from a situation (taking into account, of course, what the other person may want), you are better able to strategize together how you might achieve your ends. Intention statements generally begin with *I want, I would like,* or *I wish.*

Let's say a new project has been proposed in a meeting and you would like to head it up. The only way your boss is going to know that is if you tell her. You might say, "I'd really like to be put in charge of the Pacific Productions publicity campaign." (Clear, straightforward intention statement.) "You may not know it, but in my last job I did publicity for their major competitor, so I really know the issues." (Good documentation.) "You may already have someone else in mind, but if not, I wish you would consider me." (Showing sensitivity to the boss's possible intentions.)

It is important to be clear and direct about your intentions, so that the route to their realization is clear; but you want to be judicious in the desires that you reveal. In Chapter One, on self-awareness, we saw that learning what your intentions are often involves differentiating between hidden agendas and apparent desires. Generally, you don't want to reveal your hidden agenda. In the example above, suppose the real reason you want to head the Pacific Productions publicity campaign is because eventually you want to work for that company. Were your boss to know that intention, she might immediately begin looking for your replacement.

Your emotional intelligence comes into play here first of all by enabling you to understand what your real intentions are, then by ascertaining those it is best to divulge to others and those it is best to keep to yourself, and finally by using sensitivity in conveying your intentions.

Using sensitivity directs you to make allowances for the other person's intentions and incorporate them into your action plan. In the case of the publicity campaign, you acknowledge that your boss might have an intention different from yours, namely, someone else in mind to head up the campaign. Suppose she does. Then you might say, "Is there any way we could direct the campaign together?" This way you are still pursuing your desire, but you are compromising a bit to be able to fulfill it.

Using sensitivity also prevents you from using your intentions to influence or control others. The control element comes in when your intention is expressed as a peremptory command: "Victor, I want you to call up the client and tell him that the specs we gave him are based on last year's figures." If your real intention here is to have the client accept your bid, the best way for that to happen is to let the client know that your prices were the same last year. Think how much better Victor would feel if you phrased your intention this way: "What I wish is that the client would just accept the bid and not make us jump through any more hoops. I think if you remind him that the figures are the same as last year's, he might do that. Could you call him, please?"

Make Action Statements

These statements inform a person why you did, or will do, or are doing something, and chronicle that you did or are doing it, in case the person is unaware of the action. The importance of these statements is that they provide information that a person may not otherwise have.

For example, let's say you're in a meeting with a consultant who is presenting her suggestions for your company's reorganization and you are sitting quietly, gazing out the window. The consultant may think you are not interested in what she's saying, or that you've got more important things to think about. The reality of the situation is that you are mulling over what she has just been saying, wondering how you might implement some of her recommendations. By making an action statement such as, "I'm thinking about what you said," you clarify what was really going on, saving her the distress of thinking she was doing something wrong.

Or suppose you try all day to fax to a colleague a form he wanted but his fax line has been tied up the entire time. By telling him that—something he probably couldn't know any other way—you prevent him from thinking you are flaky or inattentive to his needs.

In the context of emotional intelligence, action statements are especially important because they let others know that you are concerned about how they might perceive your actions—or seeming inaction, in the case of the fax that can't be sent—and the impact that any misperception might have on them.

Suppose you are driving home after a meeting, and you realize that you interrupted Bill on several occasions. You didn't disagree with what he was saying or feel you had more of a right to talk than he had; you just had so much to say that you kept popping right out with it. So the next morning you say to him, "I know I interrupted you several times in the meeting yesterday, and it seemed to throw you off course. I just want you to know that the reason I did it was because I was so excited about what you were saying and had so much to say about it that I didn't show the proper restraint. It wasn't about lack of respect or disagreement, but enthusiasm." By saying this, you let Bill know that you are aware of your actions, you are concerned about the adverse effect they might have had on him, and you care about his feelings.

To make effective action statements, you must first be aware of your actions (gazing out the window, interrupting in the meeting). You may want to review the section on paying attention to your actions in Chapter One so that awareness comes easily to you. The second step is to be aware of the possible impact your action might have. A good way to do that is to imagine yourself in the other person's shoes: "I would certainly think Gerri was bored if she kept staring out the window when I was making a presentation." "I would certainly interpret Alan's not sending me the fax as an indication that he couldn't be bothered, that he didn't care whether or not I got it." "I would think Bill felt that what he had to say was so much more important than what I had to say if he kept interrupting me the way I interrupted him."

Self-disclosure is the first step in conveying to another person what your position on a particular subject is. Assertiveness is the skill you use to make sure the person gets the message.

Assertiveness

Assertiveness is the ability to stand up for your rights, opinions, ideas, beliefs, and desires while at the same time respecting those of others. In contrast to aggressiveness, which ignores the needs of the other person, and passivity, which ignores your needs, assertiveness is the emotionally intelligent way of having your needs met; it takes into account your thoughts, ideas, and feelings as well as those of the other party in a way that works to your mutual benefit.

Use Words and Body Language to Promote Your Assertiveness

Assertiveness is communicated both through the words you use and the way you use them, and through body messages. Let's look at a scenario in which your boss approaches you for the third time about working the following weekend.

YOU: I'm sorry, but I won't be able to work next weekend. As I told you three weeks ago, and then again last week, my family has plans to go out of town, and as I worked the past two weekends, this seems quite reasonable to me.

BOSS: We'd all like to have plans, but this commercial has got to be finished on time.

YOU: I know it's got to be finished on time, and that's why I'm working so hard on it. But I just won't be able to work on it this weekend.

BOSS: I know you'll be able to come through for us this weekend because you always have in the past.

YOU: I'm starting to feel frustrated because I don't think you're listening to what I'm saying. I won't be working this weekend.

BOSS: Why can't you work this weekend, which is so crucial to the project, and then take the next one off?

YOU: Because I can't just go changing the plans for my whole family. I need this time with my family to be able to regenerate so I'll be able to work even harder on the commercial next week. Look, believe me, I know how important it is that we do a terrific job on this piece. I'll come back from the weekend refreshed, I'll work late every night, and I'll come in the following weekend if it still isn't done. I won't let you down.

BOSS: OK, I can live with that.

Using this dialogue as an example of successful assertiveness, let's look at ways you can learn to use it effectively.

■■■

Tips for Using Assertiveness Effectively

1. Document your position by recalling relevant facts. You've already told your boss on two occasions that you won't be able to work this weekend, so it is important to state that you've given him plenty of forewarning. It is also important to remind him that you already worked the two previous weekends. Sometimes the other person needs to have the factual reasons behind your position underscored or recalled.

2. Acknowledge that you understand the other person's position. By telling your boss that you recognize that the commercial has got to be finished on time, and that you understand how important it is that it be great, you let him know that you are keeping his needs in mind. But you have different ideas from his as to how you'll meet those needs.

3. Use repetition. Your boss is offering a clear example of lack of emotional intelligence in trying to resolve this situation: he is trying to force his will on you. The best way to counteract that is by showing him he can't do that. Repeat to him exactly what your position is: you will not be working this weekend. Be consistent, and don't raise your voice.

4. Use feeling statements. Sometimes even with repetition the other person just doesn't accept your position and continues to try to railroad you. So use a feeling statement: "I'm beginning to feel exasperated" or "angry" or "frustrated." These are all rather powerful emotions, so if your boss hears them, he should know that he needs to take some other tack.

5. Document the reasons for your position. You need to state what's reasonable and justified about your position, and what is unreasonable and unsatisfactory about your boss's position. Although you've already explained to your boss what your reasons are for feeling justified in not working this weekend, you still need to reiterate them: you have already worked the previous two week-

ends, and you need to regenerate. What is unsatisfactory about your boss's position, in addition to what you've already mentioned, is that it means changing your whole family's plans.

6. Strive for a compromise. Your goal here should be mutual satisfaction with the resolution. You are not going to back down from your position, but you will give your boss something to make him feel pleased with the outcome: you promise you'll work late all week and the following weekend, and you assure him you'll do an even better job because you'll be refreshed by taking the weekend off.

As you put into practice each of these tips, you need to pay attention to two important considerations: first, you are aware of the messages your body is communicating, and second, you do not verge into either aggressiveness or passivity.

■■■

Make Use of Your Body Messages

We've seen how much we can convey to another person through our body language. We can use our body language to help reinforce our assertiveness.

■■■

Tips for Using Body Language to Reinforce Your Assertiveness

1. Use appropriate positioning. Stay in close proximity to the person with whom you are speaking, without getting so close that you are interpreted as being aggressive. Convey your determination: stand or sit straight, don't slouch. Lean toward the person as you speak, to suggest your eagerness to have the other person accept your position. Maintain direct eye contact, to convey your forthrightness.

2. Use appropriate facial expression. Smile when you're pleased, frown when you're angry, and furrow your brow when you're confused.

3. Keep control of your voice inflection. It's easy in a frustrating or angering situation to let your voice get louder and louder. Make every effort to keep control of your inflection, to speak in a forceful (though not enforcing), confident voice, and not to hesitate as you speak; you want to seem as rational and self-assured as you can.

■■■

Tune in to Aggressive Behavior and Passive Behavior

Sometimes, despite our best training and intentions, we find ourselves slipping into either assertiveness or passivity. Signs of the former are a raised voice, intimidating gestures or stances, and statements that disparage the other person. If you notice any of these behaviors, stop them and resort to the tips for using assertiveness effectively.

Passivity, allowing the other person to get his way, can leave you feeling angry, frustrated, or bitter. Picking up on those feelings is a good clue that you're failing to use your assertiveness. You may think, *Oh, it's best to let my boss get his way about this weekend. Then he'll like me better.* Actually, if you follow all the assertiveness tips, your boss won't feel as though you have "defeated" him, but rather that you've shown a great deal of skill in helping to lead the discussion to a mutually acceptable compromise solution.

We've looked at how self-disclosure can facilitate effective communication and how assertiveness can help in taking self-disclosure one step further. Because communication involves a back-and-forth exchange, we should also look at the other end: listening.

Dynamic Listening

Hearing is a physical sense that most of us are born with. Listening is a skill we have to learn. Dynamic listening is a practice of emotional intelligence. It brings a high degree of self-awareness into the process of understanding, acknowledging, and responding to another person. Self-awareness comes in through grasping how we allow personal filters to screen and sometimes transform information we should be receiving, and through keeping us from picking up the emotional subtext of a person's statements. In this section, we learn how to become aware of and eliminate personal filters as much as possible and how to tune in to the emotional subtext of what a person is saying.

Become Aware of Your Personal Filters

These filters are usually generated by our thoughts, ideas, and feelings. When they are turned on, they influence how much information, as well as what type of information, we hear. There are four different kinds of filters: predilection, the "who" filter, the "facts" filter, and distracting thoughts. We explore each one below and also look at some ways we can turn these filters off.

Predilection Filter

Especially in situations that produce anxiety and anger, we have a tendency to hear only what we want to hear. In some cases, this means hearing only the best of what the person has said. In others, it means hearing only the worst, because, for some reason, we want the situation to be even worse than it is.

Suppose your boss comes to you and says, "I'm really angry that in the meeting with the client yesterday you started talking about possible fees for our services. I had specifically said before the meeting that we wouldn't be discussing fees, and if I decided we should, I would be the one to do it. As far as I'm concerned, you're off this case right now. If you can come up with some plausible explanation, then I might reconsider, but frankly, I can't see any explanation, and my mind's pretty much made up."

This situation is both anger-producing and anxiety-producing. You're angry at your boss for reprimanding you, especially as the client has agreed to work with your company, but only after you said what your fee is (they expected much more). The other reason you're angry is that you have spent several months wooing the client, you know them well, and then your boss comes in at the end. What you hear is that if you come up with an explanation, you can have the client back. This is, naturally, what you want to hear. What you don't hear is that your boss says twice that you are probably off the case. What you overlook, too, is his body language: he looks you straight in the eye intently, suggesting his resoluteness, and he leans toward you almost aggressively. The message is that whether just or unjust, you're really off the case.

Now let's say you're one of those people who always see a situation in the worst possible light (perhaps the victim role is one you're comfortable with). After the same meeting (in this new scenario), your boss says to you, "Gee, I was really puzzled why in the meeting yesterday, after I had explicitly said I was the person who would reveal any figures to the client, you went ahead and did it. As far as I'm concerned, this showed insubordination and insensitivity. Unless you have a good explanation, then you're off the case."

Here your boss is definitely leaving the door open as to whether you stay on the case or not. You do have a good explanation: you know the client well, and you know they like to have figures on the table as soon as possible. Your boss is a reasonable person. But because in similar situations you (as a worst-possible-light person) just hear the threatening, negative comments, you hear now that your boss is taking you off the case, which means you probably don't have a job anymore.

Here's how you might take off this predilection filter. The method holds true whether you tend to hear just the good *or* the bad. After the encounter with your boss, go back to your office and write down everything that your boss said. Try to recall the entire conversation in its proper sequence. Jot down any notes about impressions you had at the moment: "He looked fierce" or "He seemed to be compassionate." As you review the conversation, provided that you put down what was actually said, you probably get a better picture of what was really being communicated. Then consider what you know about your boss: he tends to anger quickly and make rash decisions; he hates to be disobeyed. In the other case (the good predilection): he generally gives people a second chance; he's quite a reasonable person.

When you put all of this information together, you probably realize that in the first scenario, it's the end of your career at that company. In the second scenario, you can probably resolve things with your boss.

The Who Filter

This filter keeps us from hearing what is being said because we place so much importance on who says it. That is, what we know or think we know of the person speaking causes us to fail to hear the real message. Suppose you know your boss to be a compassionate, understanding, and reasonable person. Take the same situation of the talk of fees at the meeting with the client. Your boss comes to you and says, "This is the third time I have told you before a meeting with a client how I wanted to handle it, yet you chose to pursue your own course. This is thoroughly unacceptable to me. It shows disrespect and insubordination. You've had your last warning. You're off my staff."

Because you know your boss to be understanding, because he didn't fire you the first two times, you hear him saying that you have another chance—this is your last warning, and if you mess up again you'll be fired. What he is *really* saying is that there are no more warnings and no more chances; you're off the staff.

The critical sentence here is, "You're off my staff." But everything that you think you know about your boss keeps you from hearing it. You think he's such a fair guy that he just wouldn't fire you.

As in the case of taking off the predilection filter, you can help yourself by writing down the conversation. Here the key is to keep asking yourself, *Did he say anything else?* Hopefully, you'll remember that he said, "You're off my staff." This is a very clear message that, if you remember it, you'll have no trouble interpreting.

The who filter is especially active in situations with people with whom we have had prior negative experiences or about whom we have heard negative things said. Suppose you are working with a colleague everyone tells you is incompetent, doesn't know what she's talking about, is always poorly prepared. She comes in to discuss with you her ideas for a client's tax program. You scarcely listen to any of her suggestions, because you assume that you're just going to go ahead on your own and formulate the plan. You have developed a mind-set (*This person is an idiot*) based on what you've heard, and in the process you prevent yourself from being able to hear anything of value this person may be saying.

In such situations where you know you have a strongly preconceived notion about a particular person, tell yourself before a meeting with her that you will pay attention to everything she says and consider everything with openness and impartiality. You certainly want to take notes during the meeting, because you know you have a tendency to be dismissive of her ideas.

The Facts Filter

Sometimes all you can hear is the facts; you are oblivious to any emotive messages. Throughout this book, we've learned the importance of tuning into emotions, both your own and others'. By hearing only facts, it's easy to overlook some valuable information that emotions are conveying.

Let's take the earlier example of the production schedule that has to be shortened. An employee comes in and says, "I know how important it is to meet this new schedule. You know I've always worked extraordinarily hard and met all of my deadlines. But I am really feeling overwhelmed by the extra hours I'm having to work. I've become irritable with people because I can't get enough sleep. And I'm very sad that I see so little of my children. And I'm also afraid that we're just not going to be able to meet the deadline."

You have your fact filter on, so you say: "Well, you know we've got to meet the deadline, so just keep plugging along, and be more pleasant to your coworkers." You don't hear how distressed the employee is; all you hear is the content of what she's saying: "I know it's important to meet the deadline, I'm a hard-worker, I'm irritable." Her distress is a plea for problem solving (in the hope that you might say to her, "Let's look at any ways we might relieve the situation") or, at the very least, some understanding and sympathy ("I know how distressing this must be for you, and I really appreciate the extreme effort you're making. But I just can't see any way to change the situation.").

By not hearing the emotional content your employee is communicating, you fail to respond to her in the most effective way. To turn off this filter, use your knowledge of what feeling statements are like, and when someone uses one make note of the emotion being expressed. Here, too, it might be helpful to follow the conversation with writing down what your employee has just said, so that when you go over it you see that she says she's feeling frustrated, sad, and fearful.

Distracting-Thoughts Filter

I'm sure you've had the experience of sitting in a meeting and somehow your mind wanders off: to what you're going to have for lunch, the calls to make after the meeting, Norman's ugly bow tie, the conference taking place next week. There are many reasons why this happens. Sometimes a speaker's words come slowly, and we absorb the information faster than the flow of speech, or the speaker is boring or talks too quietly and without inflection, or we just have difficulty concentrating. Whatever the reason, a wandering mind can block out more than any of the other filters can.

One way to keep your mind on what is being said is by taking copious notes. When you have to write down what is being said, you pay attention to it; or even if you don't, you have the notes to which you can refer back. Also, use your relaxation response. This allows you to stay calm and be more attentive to the individual. If you still feel unable to concentrate, then when feasible explain to the other person that this is not a good time to meet and reschedule a time in the immediate future when it will be easier for you to listen.

In the preceding sections, we've looked at some ways to turn off the filters, such as taking notes, tuning in to feeling statements, and being impartial to "who" is speaking. Below are some other ways you can learn to become an effective listener.

∎∎∎

Tips for Becoming a Dynamic Listener

1. Summarize the speaker's statements. Sometimes doing so helps clarify that you have indeed heard what the person intends you to hear. This allows you to put into your own words what you have heard, and by repeating your summary back to the speaker you give him or her the chance to correct any misunderstanding. The following dialogue should make the process clear.

SUPERVISOR: Sometimes I think we need to offer our employees more opportunity to express their frustrations and stress. Perhaps it would help us figure out why morale has been so poor.

MANAGER: You mean that some employees need to let off steam, that it might make them feel better and work harder?

SUPERVISOR: Yes, but it's not just letting off steam. Sometimes the work becomes stressful, and they need some kind of forum in which to express themselves without fear of repercussion.

MANAGER: Kind of like a safe place to share some common concerns?

SUPERVISOR: That's right, that's exactly what I mean.

2. Use acknowledgment phrases. "I see," "Oh, really," "I'd like to hear more about it" all acknowledge to the speaker that you are listening, paying attention, and on the same track—important information for the speaker to have.

3. Acknowledge feeling statements with *I-hear* statements. In the case of the beleaguered employee toiling under the shortened deadline, you might respond to her feeling statements by saying, "I hear you're feeling overwhelmed, and this is a really difficult and unfortunate situation." "I hear you're really unhappy that you see so little of your children, and I wish we could find some way to change that." "I hear you're afraid about not meeting the deadline." These *I-hear* statements serve to clarify that you have picked up on the feeling being expressed, such that the employee might respond to your last statement, "I'm not really afraid about the deadline, but frustrated." *I-hear* statements also reassure the speaker that you understand what she's feeling, and that you care.

4. Use appropriate nonverbal cues. These serve the same purpose as phrases of acknowledgment, but they use body language rather than words. To show the speaker you are fully listening and understanding, establish direct eye contact, lean toward the speaker, and nod your head. These nonverbal cues and acknowledgment phrases shouldn't be used if in fact you're not listening but instead thinking about a memo you received earlier. Some of us are quite good at making it seem as though we're listening when in fact we're not, and this deception does not facilitate effective communication.

■■■

Tune in to the Emotional Subtext

As we've discussed in several sections of this book, people have difficulty expressing feelings. We suppress our feelings, disguise them, and hide from them—and we even cover them in facts. As an emotionally intelligent person, it is your responsibility to get underneath the facts and below the surface, to hear the feelings that are really being expressed. This is particularly important when a person is experiencing a distressful situation.

Suppose a coworker comes to you and says, "The system is so unfair." You could make inferences, such as "You mean because you didn't get the promotion?" Not only is this speculation on your part—it's possible she thinks the system is unfair for some altogether different reason—but it's not likely to be the response that she really wanted when she approached you. A better response would be, "Sounds like you're upset." This indicates that you hear the subtext of what she's saying, the real reason she wants to communicate with you. Then she'll feel more comfortable sharing her feelings with you.

When someone says to you, "My boss doesn't understand me," you could get into a discussion of how you find his boss to be an understanding man; but again your colleague is probably expressing something much deeper. An appropriate response might be, "You seem frustrated." When a coworker says, "I should have been given the promotion," the best thing for you to say is, "You seem hurt," or "You seem angry." Instead of getting into a discussion of whether or not your coworker deserved the promotion, you open the door for her to express her emotions and hopefully get some relief from the pain or anger. You can even take the process one step further by helping her with problem solving.

To tune in to the other person's feelings, use some of the same techniques as tuning in to your own feelings, namely, look at the physical and behavioral manifestations: facial expression, body language, rate of speech, tone of voice, and facial coloration (see Chapter One).

One point to keep in mind: sometimes there is no buried emotion, and the content of a statement is precisely what the person wants to communicate. Suppose a fellow engineer tells you, "This network hub is a real problem." She's probably not feeling depressed, but perplexed; what she wants is specific help with the problem at hand (how to deal with the hub).

We've seen how your emotional intelligence can be used to help you effectively disclose your thoughts, ideas, feelings, and desires; how to use assertiveness; and how to become a dynamic listener.

Now let's discuss how these skills can be constructively applied: in using criticism and engaging in team communication.

Criticism

Criticism is like a bitter pill: even though it's usually difficult and discomforting to give or receive, it is enormously helpful. Through receiving criticism, you can increase your awareness of how others perceive what you're doing, change any behaviors that don't seem to be effective, and grow through the experience. Through giving it, you help another person do the same. Just as individuals benefit from criticism, so does the organization.

Criticism is so difficult to give and receive because it usually makes the recipient feel vulnerable. It touches every aspect of your job: the quality of the work you do, how you feel about your performance, and your relationship with the person on the other end of the criticism (boss, coworker, subordinate).

Because of this vulnerability factor, people often become defensive when they receive criticism. This makes the giver of criticism approach the experience with much trepidation. Your tool for successfully giving and receiving criticism is your emotional intelligence: using your awareness of both yourself and the other person, your ability to manage your emotions, and all the communications skills we've discussed. In this section, we look at ways of making criticism productive and tips for using it most effectively, whether you're the giver or the receiver.

How to Give Criticism Productively

For this discussion, let's focus on a specific scenario: you've been working very hard on the business plan for your small graphic design firm. Your business partner is supposed to be doing it with you, but she hasn't come to the meetings you both arranged, nor has she done any of the background work she said she would. It's not a question of time, because you both have equal amounts of work to do.

Your partner also showed the same apparent lack of responsibility recently when you were writing a proposal for your major client. In both cases, you've done all the work.

Let's examine different ways criticism can be made productive.

Recognize That Giving Criticism Can Help People

The key to successfully giving or receiving criticism is acknowledging that it's a way to help her improve. With this in mind, you can see that the distressful thing has a positive goal for all concerned. This realization helps reduce both the recipient's vulnerability and the giver's anxiety. The positive purpose induces both parties to go through with it.

Make Sure That Time and Place Are Appropriate

Choose the time and the place for your discussion with care. Your criticism session is potentially embarrassing or humiliating for the person on the receiving end, so you generally want to make it as private as possible. Sometimes a neutral area is better than your office or the other person's. If your small graphics company has a meeting room, that's a good idea—but not if it has glass walls. Nor is the empty corner area with partitions that go only halfway to the ceiling. Be sensitive to comfort; it affects receptivity.

The same is true for timing. Don't schedule the meeting just before she is to meet with a prospective client, or an hour before she has to pick up her daughter in child care. When the time comes, don't carry out the criticism if you see she's in a weakened emotional state. The calmer and more relaxed she's feeling, the better she can hear what you're saying.

Protect the Other Person's Self-Esteem

Your partner may feel as though she's failed you, herself, and the business. She might feel she's incompetent, and that others blame her for the company's shortcomings. Above all, you want to protect your partner's self-esteem so that her work will not suffer. You can do this by avoiding statements that denigrate her ("You're a flake. You're a total incompetent when it comes to reports. You just can't meet your commitments."). Reinforce her self-esteem with positive statements: "You're a great designer. You do terrific work. I really like having you as my partner." By making positive statements, you enable her to see that she can change the situation. If she believes she's incompetent or a failure, then she probably can't see a solution.

Emphasize Improvement

The goal of your criticism is that your partner meet her future commitments. If you continually rehash where she has failed, she'll begin to think she's never going to meet them in the future. Discuss how your partner can work on plans and proposals next time. This indicates to her that you believe she can do them, which helps motivate her to do so, and it lets her know that you're going to continue to work with her. Using improvement-oriented criticism taps into her desire to do her best, which also serves as a motivator.

Show Concern

Throughout the session, you want to communicate with your partner that you are concerned about how she's feeling and what she's thinking. You can ask forthrightly, as though you're checking on her welfare. Your support and care reassure her that whatever mistakes she may have made, you are not turning away from her; you are there to help her.

Manage Your Own Emotions

Sometimes criticism sessions don't go smoothly, despite our best efforts. Your partner may become extremely defensive: "The reason I didn't do the business plan is that I have absolutely no time to do it. I've got too many design projects outstanding. I get all my other work done." Sometimes defensiveness leads to anger: "Besides, what are you doing getting on my case like this? Who do you think you are?" These responses will no doubt arouse your anger a couple of notches.

Practice the techniques you learned in Chapter Two for managing your emotions: using relaxation, taking time out, having a constructive internal dialogue, being aware of your behavioral actions.

There are three stages to the criticism process. Be prepared for each one to get the most benefit from the process. You need to look at what you should do before giving the criticism, during the meeting, and afterward.

■■■

Tips for Giving Criticism Effectively

Before Giving Criticism

1. Identify the particular behavior you are criticizing. You see your partner's failure to follow through on certain commitments. As you examine this, you see that your partner meets all of her design deadlines and follows through on all her other assignments and commitments. She has a problem following through on written assignments: the business plan, and the proposal.

2. Identify why it is a problem. Point out the failings: she didn't help you complete the recent business plan or the client proposal. You want to indicate the consequences: you were late completing both, because you had to do everything; both the proposal and the plan suffered from not having her insights and perspective behind them; it put a strain on your relationship.

3. Assess how best to present the criticism. Use what you know about your partner's character to assess how best to approach her with the criticism. You know she is very concerned about appearing professional in everything she does, so emphasize not what she didn't do but what the resulting plan and proposal lacked because of not having her expertise behind them. You know how much the partnership means to her, so pointing out how her behavior is compromising it helps get the message across. You know she hates being reprimanded, so be sure to present the criticism from the perspective of a problem that needs fixing.

4. Make a list of possible changes. Determine in advance what changes you would like her to make, so that you can include them as part of the discussion. Here, the change is that she follow through on what she commits to and get all the help she needs, or else not commit to doing it.

During the Criticism Process

1. Point out that you're relating your perceptions. It's a good idea to say in the beginning that these are your perceptions, and of course they are subjective: "I've been noticing that you've had difficulty fulfilling your obligations on the business plan. This has caused a number of problems for me because I've had to take the whole thing on myself, and I'm just not capable of it." (If you were to say instead, "You can't meet your obligations" or "You lack follow-through," you would be asserting that these are observable, indisputable facts; this would imply that change is difficult or impossible and would probably elicit a defensive reaction.)

2. Give specific examples that illustrate the problem. The more specific you can be, the more likely your partner will see the extent of the problem and its different manifestations. You might say: "For example, you didn't come to the meeting we arranged with the bookkeeper, to go over last year's figures. And you didn't pull together any of the information on your design projects that we needed." Make sure that these examples are used to illustrate the behaviors in question, not to give evidence proving that you are right and the other person is wrong.

3. Be sure to give positive input. Throughout the criticism, affirm the positive things your partner does: "I know you always meet the deadlines for your design projects and do gorgeous work." "I enjoy so much working with you, being your partner, and sharing this business, that I want to resolve anything that seems a problem."

4. Acknowledge the difficulty of the situation. Because you don't want your partner to feel that she's failing at something that she can easily correct, show that you understand why she may be

having difficulties: "I know that the identity project you're working on is so all-consuming, and this business plan is coming at a bad time. I also recognize that doing proposals or plans is perhaps not your thing." You're empathizing with her, which makes the criticism easier to accept.

5. Look for clues as to how she is responding. Watch her facial expressions, body language, and any other clues as to how she responds to what you say. If you see she looks perplexed, then ask her if there's something she doesn't understand. If she seems extremely upset or angry, use an *I-hear* statement to acknowledge her emotion. If she's extremely agitated, which might make it impossible for her to really take in what you're saying, then suggest that you both think over what you've already discussed and meet a little later to discuss it further. This offers a sort of cooling-off break.

6. Discuss possible solutions. One major way you can help your partner is by discussing possible solutions to the problem (you may want to review the suggestions for problem solving in Chapter Two). This way she doesn't feel she's alone, but that you are available to help her work through the situation. You might suggest she get a book on how to write a business plan, or that she be selective in accepting tasks related to such plans and take on only those she can do.

7. Reiterate the benefits to be gained. Toward the end of your talk, clarify and reiterate the benefits to be gained by your partner's making changes in how she approaches her commitment to doing reports: "We'll work better as a team, and the report will benefit from having your input." This way, in case she's in any doubt she can see that you're not giving criticism just for the sake of doing so, or to elevate your position in the relationship, that you have a positive outcome in mind.

8. End on a positive note. At the conclusion of your talk, thank your partner for doing so, reiterate how difficult it must be for her, tell

her how much you gain from this new understanding, and how much you appreciate her and enjoy working with her.

After the Criticism Meeting

1. Follow up. The most important thing to do after giving criticism is to follow up with the other person. Ask your partner how she feels about the experience, if she has any further questions, and if there is anything she doesn't understand.

2. Assess how effective the changes are. Further down the line, you may want to see how she is doing with the changes you discussed and how effective they are.

■■■

You can see that for criticism to be effective, you must walk a delicate line between expressing your concerns and being aware of how they affect the other person. To do this, as we've seen, you must put all of your emotional intelligence skills to the task. This is also true when you receive criticism.

How to Receive Criticism

It's hard to say which is the more uncomfortable position to be in: giving criticism or receiving it. I think most people agree that giving is more *difficult*, but receiving is more *uncomfortable*. It helps if you bring in your dynamic listening skills, remember how to manage your emotions, and use assertiveness techniques. Here are some ways to make being on the receiving end of criticism as useful as possible.

■■■

Tips for Receiving Criticism Productively

1. Recognize that you learn something from the criticism. This is essential to make the experience as positive as possible. If you engage in the process knowing there is a productive outcome,

then you are unlikely to fear the process and more likely to feel comfortable. You regulate your emotions with your positive appraisal of criticism.

2. Listen carefully before saying anything. This time, pretend you are the partner giving the criticism. Presumably you are aware that indeed you failed to fulfill your obligations with regard to the business plan. Before responding at all, listen carefully to what your partner has to say. If you want to remind yourself of particular responses, jot them down so as not to interrupt. Let him talk as much as he needs to.

3. Tune in to your emotions. A number of emotions are probably rising: shame that you've let the team down, embarrassment that your partner has seen your failing, frustration that your intentions to do the report and your actions never quite came together, probably a little hurt, and maybe a little anger. The first thing to do is take a few deep breaths. Notice whether you're engaging in any distorted thinking (*I'm a complete failure. Who does he think he is talking to me like this?*), and override it with constructive internal dialogue (*I am feeling upset because it's hard to hear criticism, especially for someone like me who is such a perfectionist. But I will think about what my partner is saying very carefully, and I will try to be calm.*).

4. Take responsibility for your actions. When you do reply, begin by taking responsibility for your actions. This lets your partner know that there is some common understanding—you acknowledge that there is a problem—and that you are not being defensive: "Yes, you're right, I didn't live up to my obligations for the business plan, and I'm sure that must have caused you a lot of problems. And that must also have been true with the client proposal."

5. Don't become defensive. Ensure this by listing all your reasons for not fulfilling your responsibilities. Then acknowledge your willingness to learn from the situation and improve: "I do seem to have a problem with written reports. They always stymie me.

Maybe you can tell me some ways that you go about doing them so that I won't be so resistant to doing them next time."

6. Turn off any listening filters. We learned in the section on dynamic listening how filters can screen out a lot of important information. Run through in your mind whether or not filters might be turned on here. If so, try to turn them off. Be sure to take plenty of notes so you don't miss anything.

7. Use self-disclosure statements. This is a situation where you certainly want the other person to know what you're thinking and feeling. Use interpretive statements: "I guess I expected that you would just fill in for me." Use feeling statements: "I'm feeling quite ashamed and embarrassed that I let you down."

8. Use assertiveness. This is especially useful in a situation where the criticism is not quite justified and you need to stand up for your rights, beliefs, and desires. Here, use assertiveness to underscore the message that you hate doing written reports. Perhaps you should say it more than once: "I don't like doing written reports. I think I do a lousy job with reports, but I would like to learn to do them better."

9. Be sensitive to what the criticism-giver is feeling. What you say can affect your partner on an emotional level, even though he is the one giving the criticism. For example, when you tell him that you feel ashamed and embarrassed he might feel mortified that he has caused you this discomfort. Look for signs that indicate what he is feeling, and try to make him more comfortable. You might say, "It's OK that I feel embarrassed and ashamed. You haven't caused me to feel this way; it was my own inabilities to deal with the situation properly in the first place."

10. Summarize the other person's statements. If you aren't quite sure what he has said, then use the technique we discussed in the dynamic listening section of summarizing what he says. This helps clear up any misunderstanding.

11. Show willingness to change. Presumably, change is the outcome that you both want, so indicate that you're willing to change: "You've pointed out a problem I have with written reports, and I'd really like to be able to do them. Let's talk about some ways that I can learn to do so." This leads you both to discuss possible solutions.

■■■

In the next section, we see how everything you've learned in this chapter can be put to use in group or team situations, where the dynamic is often very different from that in small meetings or interactions between two people.

Team Communication

How successfully a team, department, or group functions is directly related to how effectively the members communicate with one another in group situations. We've all been in meetings that seem magical: you could almost feel an electric energy as people share ideas, revise suggestions, support one another with enthusiasm, come up with creative and collaborative solutions, and leave feeling the department is terrific and each member of the team invaluable.

We've also been to meetings where one person dominates the discussion, people ruthlessly trounce each other's ideas, most are afraid to say anything, the discussion keeps going around in circles with nothing accomplished, and everyone leaves feeling frustrated and isolated.

What probably makes the difference is that someone (or some individuals) uses emotional intelligence to keep the meeting on a positive, forward-moving track. Although it's usually the team leader—the department head or group manager—who is responsible for guiding the tone and direction of the meeting, the responsibility is shared by each individual, because this is what teamwork is all about.

You use your emotional intelligence in group meetings to practice and encourage both self-disclosure and dynamic listening, engage in problem solving, and apply assertiveness and criticism when appropriate. The enhanced team communication that results enables the group to resolve issues, generate productive plans, and better understand how to work most effectively as a group.

How to Encourage Productive Team Communication

Many of the skills needed for effective team communication are the same ones you use when talking with just one other person, but they are more difficult to practice in a group situation. Self-disclosure can be difficult enough when face-to-face with another person, but when facing ten or twenty or more people, the desire to express thoughts and feelings can disappear in the blink of an eye. Yet self-disclosure is perhaps even more important in a team meeting. This is so because, with so many people involved, it's difficult to pick up clues as to what someone is thinking or feeling unless he or she verbally expresses it. In this section, we look at ways to encourage productive team communication.

Use and Encourage Self-Disclosure

Sometimes the best way to encourage people to do something, particularly when what you want them to do is not something they necessarily feel comfortable doing, is to actually do it yourself. Show them how in the hope that they will follow your example. This is "modeling." Suppose you're in a meeting and someone proposes a plan for merging your department with another. People ask a lot of questions about the mechanics of the merger and specifics about what the other department does. The tone of some of the questions seems a bit hostile, so you sense that people have misgivings and fears but are afraid to express them. You might say: "I'll tell you what I think. I think [interpretive statement] that by merging product marketing with direct mail we can become a lot more efficient because we can share resources and not duplicate work, as we've been doing. What I would like to see happen [intention statement] is for the merger to be as smooth as possible, with no one losing their job." Hopefully others then begin to share their thoughts and desires. If not, you can go on to ask questions: "What do you think about the two departments merging?" "What would you like to see happen to your position?"

You also want them to share their feelings, because the hostile tone suggests that they are angry and afraid. So to encourage them to open up with their feelings, you can say, "I feel a little sad that our department as we know it will no longer be the same." If other people don't start opening up, then throw out some questions: "How does this merger make you feel?" If they are still reticent, try more specific questions: "Do you fear losing your job?" "Do you feel insecure? Happy? Angry? Disturbed?"

Practice and Encourage Dynamic Listening

The department merger is a potentially unsettling situation for your team members, so perhaps they aren't terribly articulate in expressing their thoughts and feelings. Here's where summarization of what they say is helpful: "So what you're saying is you think this merger will help the other department but not ours, and you are afraid that all the job layoffs are going to come from our department?" This way you help the speaker clarify her thoughts, you enable others to understand what she is trying to say, and if your summarization is wrong you give others the opportunity to correct you.

Suppose another person says: "Well, I've got a lot of misgivings. I like things the way they were. I don't know anyone in this new department. I mean, what if we don't all like working together?" What this person really seems to be saying is, "I feel confused and unsettled." To indicate to him that you understand the emotional subtext of what he's communicating, you say, "I hear that you're feeling confused and unsettled." This opens the door for him to express what he's feeling and also indicates to him that you care about what he's feeling.

Engage in Problem Solving

Well, you definitely seem to have a problem on your hands: many people have misgivings about this new merger. So you say: "OK, we have a problem. Some people are not happy with this proposal. What do we do about it?" Then you throw open the floor for a problem-solving session: "Many people think the merger will make us less efficient. Let's look at all the good things about the merger, all the bad things, and then we'll come up with an alternative solution, if necessary." At the last stage, you suggest a brainstorming session to come up with an alternative solution. The problem solving helps the group feel as though they're working together as a team, and it also enables all of you to come up with some alternative plans you can present to upper management.

Use Assertiveness and Criticism When Necessary

Suppose you have a different idea from those of most of the others. You use assertiveness to propound your thoughts, beliefs, and opinions, following the steps we discussed earlier in this chapter. If you are the team leader and a person is assertively stating her position, but it conflicts with that of most of the other people, support her in her efforts by making sure she isn't interrupted, and even by asking questions that help draw out her assertiveness ("What factors lead you to your position? Can you be clearer about your reasons?").

Now let's say you're in a different meeting, with your editorial team and some people from design and marketing. The book that is to be the lead title among the fall releases is going to miss the deadline. The group is discussing what has gone wrong. You are the editorial director, and you say to the editor, "Michael, it seems to me you're a little too easy with your authors when it comes to deadlines. This same thing happened two years ago." The time and place for this criticism is appropriate: you are trying to ascertain what has kept the book from getting out on time, so criticism (provided that it protects his self-esteem) is in order since it emphasizes improvement as well as following all the other guidelines enumerated earlier.

In a meeting such as this, there might be plenty of criticism to go around. You say to the designer, "Marianne, I think your design was too complicated for us to be able to produce the book in time." To Ellen the marketing manager, "We told you it would be very questionable whether we could get the book out on time, but you insisted we have it for the fall." Presumably all the statements are documented, and other proper procedures for criticism follow. To ensure that the meeting doesn't turn into a blame session, keep the criticisms oriented on improvement: "How can we make our process more efficient?"

You can clearly see here that as the group gives productive criticism to one another they learn a lot about how to reduce the number of missed deadlines in the future, work better together, and communicate more effectively.

Here are some specific ways you can facilitate effective communication among the members of your team, regardless of whether you are the leader or not.

■■■

Tips for Effective Team Communication

1. Be inclusive. As you speak, talk to everyone. Move your eyes around the room; don't just focus on one person. Seek input from everyone, sometimes asking "What do you think?" of different individuals.

2. Discourage dominance. Don't allow one person to dominate the discussion, as this sometimes inhibits others from talking. You can politely say, "James, let's give someone else the opportunity to speak."

3. Be supportive. Give positive recognition. People love to hear "That's a really good idea" or "You've certainly put a lot of thought into this" or "Your evidence seems very convincing." Even if you disagree, it's sometimes a good idea to begin by saying, "I know you've considered this a great deal, but what do you think about . . .?"

4. Keep the emotional tenor at a manageable level. Some meetings have greater potential for emotional volatility than others. Questioning people's job security or performance generally falls into the higher volatility category. If people begin to yell or make irrational statements, point out that the situation is getting a little tense and perhaps a ten-minute break might is in order. You might ask questions that lead the discussion in a less emotional direction for a while.

5. Invite disagreement. Through disagreement we often learn more than we would through agreement. Often in groups there is a tendency to appear to agree, whether one truly does or not, because it seems safer. But disagreement can be productive; this suggests value in playing devil's advocate.

6. Be aware of how each member participates and responds. If you notice one person is sitting back saying nothing, you may want to try to draw him out in a way that doesn't make him feel uncomfortable. If you see that someone is becoming quite upset—perhaps criticism directed at her is not sufficiently sensitive—then intervene to protect her feelings.

■■■

Putting All the Communication Skills Together

The purpose of communication is to connect in order to exchange information (of whatever nature). In this chapter, we've looked at ways your emotional intelligence goes to work in making your interactions with others as effective as possible. From listening to disclosing, asserting to criticizing, we've seen how using your self-awareness and managing your emotions can make the difference between a successful outcome to your exchanges and a dismal one.

In the next chapter, your communication skills go to work as you learn to develop interpersonal expertise that enables your relationships to be as productive as possible.

Developing Interpersonal Expertise

Performance appraisal forms often have a category labeled "relates well to others." This trait is vitally important in work situations where relating to others often constitutes the bulk of what one does during the day. Even if you sit at your desk doing data entry, you take direction from your supervisor, answer questions from fellow data-entry personnel, collect your data from someone, and attend department meetings from time to time. All these activities involve relating to others. A person might be very smart, a hard worker, and knowledgeable in the area in question, but if he lacks interpersonal expertise, he will probably not last long in a job where he must deal with others.

In this chapter, we identify the two skills that lead to interpersonal expertise. The first is the ability to analyze a relationship. This allows you to utilize the intrinsic characteristics of the relationship to its benefit and helps you navigate a productive course through the relationship. The second skill is being able to communicate at appropriate levels so that information is exchanged effectively. But before we explore these skills, we need to begin by learning what constitutes a relationship.

What Makes a Relationship

Whatever kind of relationship we're talking about—between you and your boss; you and your secretary; you and your colleagues, clients, or customers—it covers three basic areas:

1. Meeting each other's needs

2. Relating to each other over time

3. Exchanging information about one's feelings, thoughts, and ideas

Meeting Each Other's Needs

People enter into relationships for the purpose of having one or more of their needs met. You establish a relationship with your coworker in the next cubicle because she passes on useful information and advice. The purpose of your relationship with the clerk in the mailroom is to ensure that your packages go out when you need them to go out. Your relationship with your client serves to maintain your position in your company—no client, no job. But if only your needs are being met, then the relationship is going to suffer as a result, and perhaps even end. The key to establishing a solid, productive relationship is reciprocity: you each strive to meet the other's needs. In Chapter Three, on self-motivation, we saw how important reciprocity is, for without it a relationship becomes exploitative.

In the case of your coworker, if you repeatedly seek her advice on how you should approach your boss or what you should include in the memo you are asked to write, yet never respond to her requests to help with her computer problems, then chances are she will eventually withhold her support and advice. The basis of your relationship is that she helps you meet your needs by giving advice, and you help her meet her needs by giving computer support. When you cease to do that for one another, the basis of the relationship falls out.

It is not always easy to identify what the other person's needs are. The value, of course, in identifying people's needs is that you are thus able to know what you need to do to help them meet their needs. Let's take the example of the mailroom clerk. You depend upon him to help you out in the many deadline crunches when you arrive five minutes past the deadline for a package to be sent out overnight, yet he overlooks the rules and sends your package out anyway. You learn through many such encounters with the clerk that he responds very well when you apologize profusely for the inconvenience you've caused him and heap lots of gratitude on him, telling him he's a life-saver. Assume that what he needs in the relationship is to be respected (which you do by apologizing) and appreciated (which you do by showing gratitude). Sometimes testing various responses by trial and error is the only way to learn what a person's needs are.

Dynamic listening can help, too. Ask yourself, *What is this person really saying? What does she really want?* Pay heed to her intention statements. Tune into the emotional subtext of what she's saying. Imagine being in her position and ask yourself what you might need. Empathize.

A very direct way of ascertaining what a person's needs are is to ask. Let's say you're an attorney new to your office. For the first few months, you rely upon one lawyer in particular to guide you, as she tells you how things work there and who does what. Your needs in this situation are to receive help in learning the ropes so that you can make a successful transition into your new position. You recognize that the giving is all happening on the other side (hers). But you have no idea what her needs are. You might say, "Eva, you've been so kind in helping me get on my feet here. What can I do for you? What service can I offer you?" You might even give some suggestions: "I can edit briefs really fast. Or I can help you role-play for your next trial. What are your needs?"

Identifying and responding to the needs of others is especially important in situations that call for conflict resolution and consensus building. Suppose two people you manage are both vying for a job assignment that has just come up. They've become extremely competitive with each other in meetings, and they are each trying to woo your support. As an emotionally intelligent boss, you realize that you want to come to a decision that they can each feel is reasonable; to do so, you must uncover what their needs are.

Meet them individually and ask why they want to work on the project. How does it meet their needs? Jeremy says he wants it because it's precisely the kind of work he likes to do. Daphne wants it because she feels it's a way to advance in the company. Once you identify their needs, you can more easily resolve the conflict because you know what the real issues are (and you see that they aren't incompatible). In this case, you suggest that Jeremy and Daphne work together on the project, with Daphne being the manager.

Relating to Each Other over Time

An important aspect of relationships is that they have continuity; they exist over a period of time. You wouldn't say you have a relationship with the paper supplier, whom you've called once in the last three years. But you do have a relationship with the client you meet once a month.

Continuity gives you the ability to see the other person in different situations and under different circumstances. You see your client together with her boss, without him, when she's in a good mood, when she's not, when she's fully focused, when she's a bit scattered. Each experience gives you clues to who she is, and this information helps you relate better to her. Let's say that when you first met her your client seemed rather diffident and humorless. Through many meetings, you have had the opportunity to see her interact with you and with others. You now find she can be quite open and also quite funny. But this side to her is revealed only after you and she have established rapport.

Rapport must be developed. It involves trust and comfort, both of which must be nurtured along. It enables you to know now that when your client is late it's not a sign of disrespect but of overwork. You and she feel so comfortable communicating with one another that you each confide certain things to the other about your respective companies, which exchange of information enables you to do your jobs better. The emotionally intelligent individual learns from each encounter of a relationship and uses the knowledge gained to make subsequent exchanges as fruitful as possible.

Exchanging Information About Your Feelings, Thoughts, and Ideas

Relating to another person goes beyond exchanging just factual information (the latest sales figures, the name of a contact person). It encompasses exchange of information about one's feelings, thoughts, and ideas. This exchange is an interactive process: what you disclose has an impact on the person who is listening to you, which affects how that person responds to you, and so on. By being aware of the interactivity, you learn to anticipate the responses your disclosure might generate, and you then alter your disclosure so that it best serves the relationship.

Let's say your boss, with whom you've been working for a number of years, has been short and sharp with you lately. You're not sure that he's aware of it, so you decide to share your feelings and thoughts about it. You know your boss hates it when someone tries to find personal excuses for anyone else's behavior. So even though you suspect he's been short-tempered because he's been having problems with his wife, you do not mention that; the response it would engender is probably not at all the one you are hoping for.

Instead, you say, "Jack, you know how well we've been getting along these past three years. We've always been able to talk so openly with each other." This way you reconfirm the trust you have in each other, inviting him to express what he's feeling. "Lately you've been a little sharp with me, and it's really hurting my feelings. You may not even be aware of it." You're letting him know the effect his moods have on your feelings, without challenging him or reproaching him. In response, he might say, "Gee, I wasn't aware of it. I'm so sorry I made you feel that way." Then, because you want to draw him out even more, you say, "I was just wondering if I've been doing something wrong, or doing something that has displeased you, but you're afraid to tell me." This calls for an answer; he may say, "My moods have nothing to do with you."

Because he doesn't like to bring in the personal, that's probably as far as he'll go. But you have conveyed to him that his moods are upsetting to you, and with that knowledge, he may very well alter his behavior. If you do not express these thoughts and feelings, your boss might not have a clue what's wrong, and the situation will remain the same.

If you do not anticipate some of your boss's responses, the discussion could take a very different direction. Suppose instead you say, "Jack, your bad moods are making me feel miserable. It seems I'm taking the flak for your family problems, and I don't like it." Being challenged and castigated, Jack will probably respond with hostility; his sharpness with you may very well get worse.

By anticipating the cause-and-effect nature of sharing information, especially your thoughts and feelings, you are able to guide the relationship in a positive direction, learn from experience the best way to put your thoughts and feelings into play, and grow in the relationship. Here are some ways you can make sharing your thoughts and feelings as positive as possible.

■■■

Tips for Sharing Thoughts, Feelings, and Ideas

1. Be in a good frame of mind and mood. If you are, you can be receptive to what the other person is saying, your mind is clearer for responding effectively, and you're in a better state to manage your emotions. In the preceding example, don't approach your boss when you're feeling extremely hurt or angry; wait until the feelings have subsided.

2. Tune in to how the other person responds. The better you can assess how he is responding to what you're saying, in particular what feelings you are triggering, the better you can determine how to proceed. Your assessment helps you decide what is best discussed and what is not, and how best to discuss things.

3. Set a positive tone to the discussion. You begin your discussion with Jack by telling him how well you've gotten along and how open you can be with each other; in so doing, you put him in a positive frame of mind so he is likely to be more receptive to what you're saying. You're using emotion to facilitate thought.

4. Bring out any feelings of discomfort. By discussing any such feelings, you can better manage them and bring the discussion to a more comfortable level. With Jack, you might ask him how he feels about your telling him that his sharpness hurts your feelings; this gives him the opportunity to express his own uncomfortable feelings.

■■■

Some of the thoughts and feelings that we share in the workplace have nothing whatsoever to do with the work at hand. They might concern a dreadful dinner you had at a trendy new restaurant, how your dog swallowed a jack ball and had to be rushed to the vet, your views on the ballot measures for the upcoming election, your daughter's winning a recent tennis tournament, your opinion of Martin Scorsese's latest film. Although such discussions don't help you complete the spec sheets or write the memo you must do, they do serve a valuable function: they help you forge a better relationship with the other person. By sharing your thoughts and feelings about nonwork matters, you build trust and closeness, which ultimately enable you to work together more productively and presumably more enjoyably.

Think of how much better you relate to coworkers—some of whom you may never even have spoken with before—after the company picnic or Christmas party. You see them with their spouses and children, in a different environment; you chat with them about nonwork topics, some frivolous, some significant; and when you return to work, you feel a certain connection. The same is true when you pause for a few moments while getting a cup of coffee to talk with Carl about the ball game the other evening and how his son is doing on the Little League team. These exchanges of information, though not work-related, also make up your relationships.

Now that we've looked at what constitutes a relationship, we explore how to analyze a relationship.

How to Analyze a Relationship

The good news is, you don't need to be a psychotherapist. Analyzing a relationship means examining it from different perspectives so that you can chart the best course of action, whether for a specific encounter or for the long-term relationship. The skills you need to practice analysis are awareness of the other person's feelings, moods, and needs; and your appraisals of different situations. Here are the steps to analyzing a relationship:

1. Know the relationship boundaries.
2. Consider relationship expectations.
3. Examine your perceptions of the other person.
4. Ascertain the other person's perceptions of you.
5. Examine specific encounters.
6. Determine desired relationship outcomes.

Know the Relationship Boundaries

Relationship boundaries are often unspoken: you don't know they're there until you transgress them and are denounced for doing so. Take the example of your boss, Jack, who lets it be known that personal excuses don't belong in work relationships. There are probably consequences to crossing that boundary—Jack's displeasure and even anger. Unless you've set the boundaries, then you don't have the power to change them, and this can be quite difficult to accept.

The emotionally intelligent person respects relationship boundaries but also looks for ways around them. The conversation with Jack is a good example. You don't mention Jack's marital problems, nor do you pursue the point by asking, "Well then, what's causing you to act like that?" when he perfunctorily says, "My moods don't have anything to do with you." By asking questions that skirt the boundary, you get what you want from the conversation: Jack's understanding of how his moods affect you.

Sometimes you can't find a way around a boundary. It then seems to be a real barrier to having a productive relationship. Suppose you feel stymied in establishing a good understanding with Jack because of his policy of not wanting personal problems to be brought up at work. You might try to talk directly with him about this.

Let's say your son has gotten in with the wrong crowd at school and has been caught shoplifting. You have grounded him but you don't trust him. Not only is this causing you a great deal of anxiety, but you have to call home several times each afternoon. You hope that if you explain to Jack what's going on, he will be sympathetic and relieve you of some afternoon meetings so you can be available to check up on your son. You might approach Jack by saying: "Look, I know how much you hate it when people bring up stuff that's happening at home, but I have something really important to share with you that does involve what's going on at home, and it would really mean a lot to me if you would allow me to discuss it with you." If Jack is at all reasonable, then he will accept your request. If he's not, and doesn't, then ask yourself how comfortable you are in the relationship, how important openness is to you. If the relationship is making you too uncomfortable, and if it's not meeting your needs, then it may be time to look for another position in the company—but only after you make every effort to rectify what you find is wrong about it.

Consider Relationship Expectations

We often want more from a relationship than it is reasonable to expect. You want your boss to teach you everything she knows. You want your assistant to be able to read your mind. You want your client to keep you informed every day. When expectations go beyond what the other person can possibly do, then we become disappointed and frustrated, and sometimes angry—emotions that tend to work against productive relationships. By looking at previous experiences and by seeking advice from others, we can often get a reality-based check on our expectations.

Suppose you expect your sales rep, who comes to you with glowing recommendations, to bring in orders that exceed anything your existing staff has been able to accomplish. To assess whether or not your expectation is realistic, you may want to look at the past to predict the future. Even though your new rep got million-dollar orders at his old company, the circumstances were very different. Furthermore, no matter how hard your other reps have worked, they have just not been able to pull in any million-dollar orders. So you might assume that your expectations are not realistic; to preserve your good relationship with the rep, you need to revise them.

Sometimes it's helpful to seek the advice of another person, as oftentimes we cannot be sufficiently objective in relationships. Let's say your expectation in taking your current job was that your boss would teach you what she knows. But so far, she has done little of that, and you're extremely disappointed. So you ask a coworker what she thinks. She says that your boss recently took over much of another person's job and probably has little time to "teach" you. But when something isn't clear, or when you think you could do something so much better with a little guidance, consider asking your boss if she has a few minutes—say, to explain to you how she puts together her cold-call list.

Examine Your Perceptions of the Other Person

This involves using your appraisal skills, which we discussed in Chapter One. We saw there how our appraisals are influenced by various factors that shape our personalities, including family background, previous experiences, natural abilities and inclinations, and systems of belief. In looking at how you perceive others, you need to ask yourself if you're being as objective as possible, or if these formative factors are causing you to see the other person in a biased way.

Suppose you've been having problems getting along with your assistant. She doesn't seem to be doing what you ask her to do; nor does she come to you for advice. Ask yourself what your perceptions of her are. You find that, frankly, you don't think she's up to the job; you find her a bit arrogant. Your previous assistant, George, was terrific. But when you look fairly at what he did and what she does, you realize there is really not that much difference. Yet your belief that men can generally do jobs better than women keeps you from seeing Eileen as she truly is: a reasonably competent assistant who is still learning about the job. As for why she doesn't come to you for advice, you might realize that you're really not the nurturing, helpful type; perhaps this, not her arrogance, is what keeps her from seeking your advice.

As you can see, by carefully examining your perception of the other person you gain invaluable insights that you can use to help put the relationship on the best track. You learn about the other person, yourself, and the relationship itself.

Ascertain the Other Person's Perception of You

Just as you have certain notions and expectations about others, they have their own perceptions about you. How they perceive you often affects how they respond to you. If you are perceived as competent and knowledgeable, then another person is likely to accept and respond favorably to what you say; if you are perceived in the opposite way, then chances are your ideas will be challenged and questioned.

Sometimes the only way to ascertain what a person's perception and expectations of you are is through analyzing the responses you engender. Suppose in meetings you tend to be extremely opinionated—though you're not fully cognizant of it. You might figure it out when, after you've expressed your opinion for the umpteenth time, your boss says, "We've heard all about your opinions; let's listen to what someone else has to say."

Another way to find out is by asking someone. Let's say you suspect you might be too opinionated, but no one has said anything to you (and you miss the eye-rolling that takes place when you blurt out your opinion yet again). You say to a coworker, "I have something a little delicate to ask you, but I want your honest answer. Am I too opinionated?"

If you are not pleased with the response you get from another person or the outcomes that ensue, then consider those consequences to be a clue that you need to see what you can do to alter people's perceptions of you. Saying "I'm just opinionated, that's who I am" is not going to enhance any of your relationships. But by trying to withhold some of your comments, or by asking others what their opinions are, you help them regard you more favorably, which ultimately makes your relationships more productive.

Sometimes you have little information on which to base your assessment of others' perceptions of you. This is especially true in first-time encounters through which you hope to establish long-term relationships. Yet this is precisely the time when you want perceptions of you to be most favorable. Let's say you're meeting with a potential client. You have heard that he is very exacting, a stickler for detail, and insistent on getting his own way. To help ensure that he takes away a favorable impression of you, come to the meeting extremely well prepared, with all your facts in order. Since you know that he likes getting his way, don't argue with him over a point on which he disagrees with you. Instead, send him documentation supporting your position later, with a note saying, "Thought you might be interested in seeing this."

Examine Specific Encounters

Sometimes the best way to understand a relationship is to see it through a specific encounter between you and the other person—view the encounter as though you are an impartial observer, not a participant. Essentially, you replay the exchange in slow motion, freeze-framing it for a closer look at key moments.

Let's say you normally have a very productive and pleasurable relationship with your coworker, but lately you sense some tension. You review the last meeting you had with her, at which you discussed the product release of the new modem software that you're working on, to see if there were any clues. Roll the film, in slow motion. You're in the meeting, and you check in with each other on what you have been doing. She becomes a little testy when you ask if she's going to be able to get her contribution to the prototype in on time. You feel impatient with her when she reveals she is falling behind. You must be conveying this to her, because as you talk about what you have been doing she isn't paying much attention. This annoys you, and you say sarcastically, "I'm glad you're so interested." When your boss comes in to the meeting to see how the project is going, your coworker misrepresents what she has been doing. When he leaves, she abruptly ends the meeting, saying she has important calls to make.

In reviewing the encounter, it's helpful to ask yourself some questions:

Did I listen well? Communicate well?

Did the other person listen well? Communicate well?

How do I perceive the other person's behavior during this encounter?

How does the other person perceive mine?

Did the encounter go the way I wanted it to?

What might I have done differently?

What might the other person have done differently?

Did I reach a new level of understanding about the relationship?

Did the other person?

In applying these questions to your exchange with your coworker, you see that you didn't listen well. When she became testy about whether or not she was going to make the deadline, you could have said, "I hear you're a little worried about meeting the deadline." That way she might have conveyed her real feelings, and then you could have perhaps engaged in some problem solving. Nor were you communicating well. The sarcasm made her angry. But she also listened and communicated poorly. She could have disclosed her thoughts and feelings: "I'm afraid I won't be able to meet the deadline." "I think it was a mistake that I was given the tasks I was, because you're much better at doing them." "It seems to me that you're trying to take over this project."

The encounter did not go the way you wanted it to. What you really wanted, and still do, is for you both to be enthused and fired up to continue working on the project. But you have gained a few insights about the relationship. You need to communicate better with one another, both in disclosing what you're feeling and thinking, and in listening—especially tuning into the emotional subtext of what the other person is saying. You also think your coworker might be feeling competitive with you—hence her misrepresenting to your boss how much she had done. You need to work on being less competitive with one another and more supportive.

Determine Desired Relationship Outcomes

In analyzing a relationship, it's always a good idea to figure out what you want from the relationship. This is not a question of having your needs met, though of course that is part of it, but of determining what your goal for the relationship is, what outcome you want it to have. By knowing that, you're in a much better position to ascertain whether or not you're on the right course and, if not, how to change direction to get there.

Let's pursue the preceding example and suppose that what you would like to get out of the relationship is good modem software products that result from a truly collaborative effort. Right now, you're off course, because you're not collaborating but competing. So you need to look at all the steps you can take to get to your objective.

The desired outcomes, from the relationship point of view, might be that you offer each other motivational support, share expertise, exchange contact lists, or serve as sounding boards to one another. Each outcome has a different path; by determining the outcome, you can figure out the path. For example, if you decide that you desire a client relationship that generates work, then you certainly should be pleasant with the client; but you don't need to share personal stories the way you would if you wanted your client for a friend (unless, of course, sharing personal stories makes the encounter more pleasant).

We've seen the invaluable information that relationship analysis gives you about yourself, the other person, and the relationship, and how you can use that information, along with your emotional intelligence, to make of the relationship what you want it to be. Now we look at another way you can guide the relationship to its desired outcome.

How to Communicate at Appropriate Levels

You've probably experienced having a conversation and feeling that you and the other party are talking at cross-purposes, say, one of you discussing modem software and the other talking about the new organization chart. Often, one person is communicating niceties ("Hi, how ya doin'? Great weather!") and the other person might be communicating feelings ("I'm very distressed about where I fit in on this new org chart."). You can see here that the difference in levels at which each person is communicating makes meaningful discussion rather difficult; any kind of connection between the two individuals is almost impossible.

It is connection that is so important in relationships, as we discussed earlier, because connection gives depth, meaning, and value to the relationship. Communication helps establish connection, and connection makes communication easier. Both are facilitated by such emotional intelligence techniques as self-disclosure, criticism, dynamic listening, awareness, and assertion.

The goal of interpersonal expertise is to establish peak communication with another person. This means that the individuals involved are perfectly in sync, fully attuned, and totally connected. They are completely comfortable in sharing thoughts, feelings, and ideas and know they are listened to accurately. By feeling such an extreme level of comfort, the individuals can be more creative in their thinking and more enthusiastic about sharing their feelings. Needless to say, few achieve this level of communication, either in work or in personal relationships; yet it is certainly something to strive for.

There are four levels of communication beneath this peak level—and all are manageable:

1. Niceties
2. Factual information
3. Thoughts and ideas
4. Feelings

Your emotional intelligence comes in by knowing how to use each level to connect most effectively, and by encouraging others to shift to levels they might wish to avoid but that will keep the relationship moving ahead and the individuals connecting more closely.

The Niceties Level

This first level encompasses the pleasantries you exchange with someone as you pass in the corridor or see that individual in the cafeteria. "Good morning" and "How are you?" and other salutations are examples. This level of communication serves to acknowledge the other person's presence, without going beyond the initial greeting. The speaker usually doesn't expect a response and often doesn't listen if one is given. Although this level of communication serves legitimate purposes, the *connection* it establishes is of the flimsiest nature.

The difficulty here is that sometimes a person responds on a different level. Suppose you pass your friend Daniel from the MIS department and he says, "Hi, how are you?" You reply, "I'm glad you asked, because I've got a problem." He says, walking quickly past, not having heard your reasons, "That's nice, hope to have lunch with you soon."

Were Daniel an emotionally intelligent individual, he would know that every response needs to be listened to, even one as cursory and cryptic as "I've got a problem." Not only would Daniel recognize there is an emotional subtext here that he needs to tune in to, but he would see that you are switching levels of communication, and he should do the same.

Suppose your coworker passes by, you ask "How's everything going?" and she says, "Everything is fine." But you pick up from her low tone and slow, dispirited walk that she is feeling dejected or frustrated. Remember that feelings are expressed not just through words but through behaviors as well. Your emotional intelligence leads you to say, "I'm hearing that everything *isn't* fine. Would you like to go somewhere and talk about it?"

Pay attention to all the emotional transmitters that accompany this level of communication—tone of voice, facial expression, body language, and speech pattern—rather than simply taking the spoken words at face value. Use the information that your awareness gives you to ascertain how others are feeling.

■■■

Emotional Intelligence at Work

I was a graduate student at a large university and was feeling so down because one teacher was giving me a really tough time and I just didn't think I could make it through the semester. I was in the hallway, hoping I would run into him, when another teacher passed by. "Hey, how ya doing?" he asked. He continued whisking down the hallway, but I yelled, "Terrible!"

He stopped, walked all the way back, and asked me what was wrong. He listened patiently and then told me to come see him the next day and we'd make a plan of action. The fact that he came back to talk to me was really uplifting and left me feeling that I might make it through the semester after all. (Andy B., management consultant)

■■■

Factual Information Level

The business of business is often the exchange of information of a factual nature, whether it's to report the latest sales figures, present the new organization chart, review the monthly plan, teach the new word-processing program, or set departmental goals. But each of these exchanges engenders a positive, negative, or close-to-neutral perception of the facts, perceptions that can then trigger a corresponding emotional response.

Sales figures are just numbers, but they can bring happiness to some people (those who are responsible for the numbers being so good) and anxiety to others (those who didn't meet their individual sales goals). The monthly plan brings relief to some people (those who are already ahead of the game) and depression to others (those who just can't figure out how to get everything done). Even learning the new word-processing program can cause some people to feel like idiots and others like computer whizzes.

Again, the emotionally intelligent person recognizes that there's an emotional component even to the factual level of communication, and it's the responsibility of the person presenting the facts to note how the facts are being interpreted. By the same token, the person listening to the facts can note how they are being presented and make certain deductions as to how the presenter feels about the facts. If, in presenting the departmental goals, the manager stutters a bit, hesitates a lot, and looks down at the floor, the listeners could infer that he doesn't feel comfortable with the goals, has misgivings about how they will be interpreted, or doesn't think the department is up to the challenge. (Of course, he could also simply be nervous speaking before the whole department; part of emotional intelligence is to identify and eliminate that possibility.)

Once you detect the emotional content, then you have the option of dealing with it, whether to reassure the nervous word-processing student that he is indeed able to master the program, or to let the departmental manager know that you feel confident of meeting the goals.

Some factual communications are especially highly charged. Take the case of a performance appraisal, where the manager is communicating the "facts" of performance. Inevitably, emotions surface in this situation: fear, anxiety, embarrassment, and others. If the two people can't go beyond the factual level in this communication, then they come up against a barrier to further understanding. If, however, the manager deals with the emotional aspect, for example by acknowledging that the subordinate may feel angry at getting such a poor performance appraisal, then the two have a much better chance of using their new knowledge to benefit the relationship. The manager might say, "I hear that you're angry about the appraisal" or "I can understand that this must be rather upsetting to you, but we can discuss ways that you can improve, and I'll be there to help you." By addressing the employee's concern about the facts, the manager makes the facts more acceptable to the employee.

Thoughts and Ideas Level

This level introduces a greater degree of vulnerability, because we all have a certain investment in our thoughts and ideas—unlike straight facts—and fear that our ideas will be rejected or our thoughts dismissed as unworthy.

Suppose an employee comes to you and says she has a great story idea for the next issue of the magazine. She explains it to you. You don't think it's a great idea. Here's the emotionally intelligent way of handling your response: "I really appreciate it that you keep coming up with new ideas, Maureen, because it shows your interest and enthusiasm, and by sharing ideas, that's how we come up with the best issues. I don't think this particular one will work, even though it's a good one, because we're getting away from interior design stories. But the next idea of yours might work. Please keep them coming."

Think of how different Maureen's response would be if instead you say, "I can't agree with you that that's a great story idea, because, as you should know, we're not doing interior design features any more." The consequences of this interaction may be loss of trust (Maureen might no longer feel comfortable sharing her ideas), loss of self-esteem (she probably feels she showed stupidity and incompetence), and loss of resources (the magazine loses out on her creative input).

The first approach shows emotional intelligence: you protect Maureen's vulnerability by using sensitivity in your response, and you support and encourage her to keep coming up with new ideas.

Here's an example of making the best use of an exchange of thoughts. Let's say you're in an editorial meeting and Tom says, "I think the magazine has been devoting too many pages to interior design stories." You disagree but say, "What are your reasons for thinking that?" Tom replies, "The photography is expensive and time-consuming, and the stories tend to be boring." You say, "I certainly agree with you there, but those features bring in a lot of advertising dollars, and I just don't think, given our current situation, that we can afford to turn our backs on that money."

If you lacked emotional intelligence, you might instead say, "That's really dumb, Tom. You know how much advertising money those stories bring in and how much we need it."

The first response protects Tom's vulnerability, shows there is some agreement, and leaves room for other people's thoughts by saying, "I just don't think we can turn our backs on that money." By arguing with Tom, in the second example, you set up a confrontational situation with defensive behaviors, and no hope for a productive outcome.

By presenting your disagreements as a different course to take or another option to look at rather than the best and only course, not only do you help the other person feel comfortable sharing thoughts and ideas now and in the future but you enable that person to consider more openly the other thoughts and ideas proposed, even those that are contradictory.

Feelings Level

Each level we go up on the way to the peak level of communication involves more risk, but also more reward. This is especially true of feelings. We've discussed in other chapters, and earlier in this, one reason why communicating feelings is so difficult: we're unaccustomed to doing it, we fear possible repercussions, and it makes us feel vulnerable. Yet it is precisely through sharing feelings that we become much more connected to other persons. We reveal an intimate part of ourselves, which enables them to know us better, and us to know ourselves better. We unburden ourselves of something that is often troubling, and in exchange we find help in the form of support and problem solving. And we each demonstrate our trust in the other person. All of this brings individuals closer to one another.

In the section on self-disclosure in Chapter Four, we looked at how to disclose your feelings, and in this chapter we looked at how to share them. A point to remember is that you often elicit communication at the feelings level by initiating it yourself. By doing so, you make it clear that expressing feelings is acceptable and advisable. For example, your staff is discussing the mechanics of the newly proposed organization chart and ideas for revising it. What you really want them to discuss is their feelings about it. So you say, "I'm feeling really enthusiastic about these changes, and I'd like to know how you feel, especially as I sense some discomfort."

We've identified the four levels of communication, and we've seen that as an emotionally intelligent person we want to strive for the peak level, which incorporates all four levels and the fullest use of each. In the next section, we explore how to make the most productive use of the different levels.

How to Use the Different Levels Effectively

As we've seen, a particular level of communication is appropriate in certain circumstances, while another one is not. Sometimes you're communicating at one level, but it seems another would be more appropriate. To use the different levels of communication most effectively, you must be able to identify the levels you and the other person are each at, match your level to the other person's, and know when to move to a different level.

Identify the Level You Are Each At

As we've just seen, each level has certain characteristics. Niceties usually involve greetings and salutations. The factual information level covers the facts, just the facts. The thoughts and ideas level is characterized by statements beginning with "I think" or "A good idea might be." The feelings level usually involves statements of the *I-feel* nature. By understanding each level, and then by using your self-awareness, you should be able to determine at which level you and the other person are each communicating. Tune in to all the behavioral clues, because often the words seem to indicate one level ("*I think* this new schedule is all wrong" suggests the thoughts level) while behaviors suggest another (the words are yelled, suggesting anger or frustration, which comes from the feelings level).

The value of being able to identify which level you're at is to ascertain when you and the other person are both at the same level. If you're not, the resulting communication suffers. If the other person shares his thoughts and ideas on the new organization chart while you say how distressing it is for you because you don't see any room for you to advance on it, he's not going to get what he wants (your own thoughts and ideas on the subject, and comments on his) and you're not going to get what you want (help figuring out how you might deal with the unfortunate situation). Effectively, you're not connecting.

By becoming aware of yourself operating at each different level, you get to know which levels are more comfortable for you and which you tend to avoid. Because to establish productive interpersonal relationships you need to utilize all the levels at their appropriate times, it is a good idea to learn what causes you discomfort at a particular level and how you can work through it. The more you use a particular level, the more comfortable you feel using it.

Match Your Level to the Other Person's

When you match your level of communication to the one at which the other person is communicating, you exchange similar kinds of information and have a common frame of reference. This makes it possible for you to hear what the other person is saying, understand it, and respond in a way that benefits you both; you connect and relate well.

Matching communication is a fluid process. We continually change levels for a variety of reasons, as we discuss shortly. Because a connection takes place only when both individuals are communicating at the same level, if the other person switches to another level, you need to follow suit, and vice versa.

People generally shift down to a lower level of communication, a less risky one, when the one they're in becomes uncomfortable. Maureen presents her interior design story idea, only to be told it's a bad idea because the magazine isn't doing those kinds of features any more. The rejection of her idea may very well make her feel uncomfortable continuing to communicate at the thoughts and ideas level, and it probably makes her unwilling to risk having another idea put down. She certainly doesn't want to make herself more vulnerable by shifting up to the feelings level, so most likely she'll shift down to the factual level. She might say, "As we're not doing interior design stories, will we be doing more fashion or lifestyle features?" The listener, if emotionally intelligent, changes levels with her, perhaps discussing the kinds of stories on which they'll be focusing.

Suppose Maureen has some other ideas she would like to discuss. The best thing would be for her to stay in the factual information level until she regains a sense of comfort, and then try moving back up to the ideas level.

Know When and How to Move to a Different Level

The time to move to a different level of communication is when you recognize that the level you are at is not effective. This might be because the other person is at a different level, because the level you are at is causing discomfort to you or the other person, or because you think the informational exchange would be better served at a different level (say you and a coworker are discussing thoughts and ideas about your new product launch, but you're getting nowhere, so you decide to switch to the factual level to get some clarity). Another time that switching levels is called for is when feelings aren't being verbally disclosed yet are really the operating factor; switching to the feeling level may help establish a better connection.

As for how you move to a different level and take the other person with you, there are four approaches:

1. Use self-disclosure statements.
2. Ask strategic questions.
3. Solicit thoughts and feelings.
4. Solicit thoughts and feelings about expressing thoughts and feelings.

Suppose you and your colleague Ron are going over an important presentation you are about to make to a potential client. He keeps reviewing the facts with you. From his pacing back and forth and his hesitant speech pattern, you sense that he is anxious. In the following sections, we refer to this example as we learn to use each of these approaches for moving to a different level of communication.

Use Self-Disclosure Statements

Although Ron is communicating at the factual information level, your senses tell you that his real concern is the feelings he's having—

anxiety and nervousness—rather than his command of the facts. So to elicit a discussion of what he's feeling, make a self-disclosure statement ("I sense," "I think," "I feel," "I wish"). In the previous chapter, we saw that generally when one person leads the way in self-disclosure, the other follows suit. Also, people usually welcome the opportunity to discuss a distressful emotion with a coworker, if they feel safe doing so, and let's presume Ron feels safe with you.

In this case, your self-disclosure statement might be, "Ron, I'm sensing that you're somewhat anxious about this presentation. Want to talk about it?" You disclose to Ron that you have picked up on his anxiety, and by so doing, you open the door for him to talk about it, thereby moving up to the feelings level. You could also say, "I think it might be a good idea if we did some deep breathing to get rid of some anxiety." Ron might say, "Good idea. I am feeling really anxious." Or you can say, "I'm feeling just a little bit anxious about this presentation." Hopefully Ron then picks up on your invitation to discuss what he's feeling and discloses his own anxiety.

The value of moving up to the feelings level is both short-term and long-lived. Ron gets short-term relief in the form of help in feeling less anxious. You both benefit in the long run by having this experience of expressing your feelings, noting the positive outcome that ensues, and then being able to find it easier to use this level of communication in the future.

Ask Strategic Questions

Sometimes a question is the way to help someone move to another communication level. Say to Ron, "How are you feeling about this upcoming presentation?" He tells you that he's feeling nervous, and you then ask him if there's anything you can do to relieve his anxiety.

On the other hand, Ron might respond to your question by saying, "Fine." Your senses tell you that this is not true, so you might use a self-disclosing sense statement ("I sense that you're a bit anxious."). If he asks you what leads you to say that, then you have your sense data (his pacing, his jerky speech) as documentation.

You might also try combining a self-disclosing statement with a strategic question: "I'm feeling kind of anxious about this presentation. What about you, Ron?" By letting Ron know that you are feeling the same thing that he is, you make it easier and safer for him to disclose his feelings.

Solicit Thoughts and Feelings

The best way to do this is to offer your services as a dynamic listener. You do this by incorporating "I would like to hear" into a statement: "Ron, I'd really like to hear how you're feeling about this presentation." Like most people, he probably responds to the solicitation for a feeling response with a thought (remember that in Chapter Four we discussed how people often confuse an *I-think* statement with an *I-feel* statement). He'll probably say, "I think we're pretty much on top of things, so it should go OK." You might reply by saying, "I'm really asking about your feelings, not about your thoughts." If he still doesn't get it, you could ask, "Are you feeling anxious? Confident?"

If it's thoughts you want someone to share, so you can shift to the thoughts and ideas level, then you can say, "I'm sure you have some ideas about the best way to begin the presentation, Ron. I'd like to hear what they are."

Solicit Thoughts and Feelings About Expressing Thoughts and Feelings

Sometimes, despite your best efforts, you are unable to shift the communication to the thought or feeling levels. Rather than insisting or relenting, encourage the person to deal with the resistance by speaking about it.

Here's how this might work with Ron. Suppose he just can't discuss his anxiety with you. You say, "It seems to me that it's difficult for you to share your feelings with me. Perhaps it's something I'm doing and am not aware of. How do you feel about my asking you this?"

Ron probably feels safe responding to that last question, so he might say, "I feel a little embarrassed" or "A little uncomfortable" or "Fine." You then ask, "Do you feel uncomfortable or embarrassed talking about your feelings in general?" He says, "No, I feel scared." In effect, you have gotten Ron to shift to the feelings level by revealing to you how he feels about expressing his feelings. Once you're at that level, try to bring the discussion back to the presentation. "Do you feel scared about the presentation?" Hopefully Ron remains at the same level in giving his reply.

The following is some advice about when it's a good idea to shift levels and when it isn't.

■■■

Tips for Knowing When and When Not to Shift Levels

1. Shift to a factual information level if someone is extremely angry. This way you can diminish the emotional intensity, put the anger in perspective, and deal with the anger more productively. Suppose Charles, a coworker, comes into your office furious that he was passed over for a recent promotion. Instead of using *I-hear* statements ("I hear how upsetting this must be for you") designed to draw out feelings, ask relevant fact-seeking questions ("But hasn't James worked in this department much longer than you?") or make factual comments ("But don't forget, your boss told you he was grooming you to head his upcoming pet project."). This way your coworker looks at "the facts" of the case, perhaps gaining new insights that help reduce the anger.

2. Shift to a feeling level when someone communicates despondency nonverbally. Let's say a friend from a different department communicates with you at the niceties or factual level. When you run into her in the corridor and ask how she is, she replies, "Fine" (niceties). When you have lunch with her and ask how everything is going, she tells you what tasks and projects she's working on (facts). But she seems downcast: she tries to avoid talking with you, she doesn't smile anymore, she doesn't look you in the eye. By helping her move to a feeling level, you can get her to talk

about her despondency, and together you might figure out what she can do to alleviate it.

3. Don't shift out of a thoughts or feelings level if building trust and consensus is your goal. To build trust and reach consensus, you need to establish openness and honesty. Sharing thoughts, ideas, and feelings is a way to do that. By staying at these two levels of communication, you maximize your chances for gaining trust and reaching consensus.

4. Don't shift out of the factual or the thoughts and ideas level when you're doing problem solving. Let's take the case of your colleague Charles, who wasn't given a promotion and is extremely angry. Anger indicates a problem, and you graciously agree to help Charles find a solution that will leave him feeling more comfortable with his boss's decision. So you explore the facts of the case and offer thoughts and ideas. If you shift to the feelings level, Charles won't be able to see clearly enough to come up with any positive actions.

5. Don't shift out of the niceties level if you're not prepared to have a more meaningful exchange. When a coworker comes into your office wanting to have a discussion, but you are preoccupied with a report due that afternoon, keep your communication to an exchange of pleasantries; otherwise you imply to him that you are prepared to have a talk at a higher level. It's also a good idea to tell him that you would really like to talk with him about what's on his mind, but you can't until the report is in. That way you let him know that your inability to move to a different level is only temporary, and that you really are a sensitive person.

6. Generally, don't shift to a level different from the other person's if she is in a position of power or control. Let's say your boss or client is communicating at the factual level, but you think you could advance the discussion by shifting to the thoughts and ideas level. Only do so if you are convinced she won't take offense. Your boss might think you insubordinate if you offer your

opinions when they aren't solicited; your client might think you insensitive if you jump in with your ideas when it's hers that should take precedence. On the other hand, they might both be open-minded and eager to hear your thoughts and ideas. But bear in mind that there may be risks to changing communication levels in these situations.

■■■

As we've seen in the preceding section, the higher the level of communication you use, the better you relate to one another, with the proviso that lower levels are sometimes more appropriate in certain circumstances. Because self-disclosure statements are a good way to reach those higher levels, and because those statements are usually responded to in kind, you can easily extrapolate that to get closer to the peak level of communication use self-disclosure statements early on in a relationship, guide many of your exchanges to the thoughts and ideas and the feelings levels as soon as possible, and try to remain there.

■■■

Emotional Intelligence at Work

Not too long ago, I was preparing to give one of my employees his performance evaluation—not one of my favorite tasks. In the first two appraisals I had given him, he was pretty silent. I was determined not to let this happen again.

I tried to figure out the reasons for his silence. Maybe he felt threatened, or maybe he just thought the whole process was a big waste of time. Perhaps he really had nothing to say, or thought I would ignore his input. I thought he must have *some* things on his mind, and if I could get them to surface, the evaluation would be much more productive for both of us.

Before the meeting, I told him to set aside ninety minutes. I thought that was a good way to let him know the evaluation was not going to be brief. I also told him I would ask him to give *his* evaluation of his performance. This let him know that he would have to participate.

After we exchanged niceties and he seemed a bit more relaxed, I suggested we begin with his self-evaluation. I told him that for us to benefit from the discussion, I would need to know what he thinks.

Right off the bat, he seemed overly cautious in expressing his views. So I asked him to elaborate on his points. I asked questions like, "Could you tell me a little more?" "Could you give me an example?" "What do you think is the best plan to take?" He became a little more expressive, and I gave him positive reinforcement, especially when he shared his thoughts and feelings, by saying things like "I appreciate your input" or "That's insightful." Periodically I paraphrased and summarized what he was saying, asking if I was getting his message. I wanted him to feel he was being listened to.

I followed the same process when I spoke. I asked for his thoughts about what I was saying, and when he disagreed, instead of getting defensive, I asked him to elaborate to clarify his own thinking. Whatever disagreements there were, I found that by getting him to express his own thoughts and feelings we were able to create an accurate appraisal of his performance.

We both thought the session was terrific. As he was leaving, I told him that I really appreciated his input, and he could see that I did. The next day, I reiterated my appreciation. Ever since, he has been much more expressive with his thoughts and feelings in dealing with me, and we have a much more productive relationship. (Sondra L., manager of an auto parts supplier)

■■■

Putting All the Interpersonal Expertise Skills Together

In this chapter, we've seen how interpersonal expertise is crucial to developing and maintaining the best relationships you can have with all those you encounter during your workday. (Incidentally, the skills you've learned here translate very well to your life beyond work as well.)

We've also seen the key role that your emotional intelligence plays in helping you to develop interpersonal expertise: it gives you the awareness you need to analyze your relationships; it enables you to manage your emotions so encounters at all levels of communication are as productive as possible; and it gives you the communication skills—from self-disclosure to dynamic listening and assertiveness—that allow you to connect with another person meaningfully and appropriately.

In the final chapter, we take this expertise one step further and use it to help others help themselves—one of the most difficult and rewarding practices of emotional intelligence.

6

Helping Others Help Themselves

A work organization is a holistic entity, an integrated system that depends upon the interrelationship of the individuals who are part of it. How each person performs affects the company as a whole. That's why it's so important to the success of the company not only that all employees perform to the best of their abilities but that they also help others do the same. In the context of emotional intelligence, this means helping others to manage their emotions, communicate effectively, solve their problems, resolve their conflicts, and be motivated. Collectively, these skills are called **emotional mentoring.**

It Benefits Others, You, and the Company

We've seen how learning to use our emotional intelligence in the workplace is a process that requires time and a good deal of practice. We must learn new skills, and we may need to relearn how to do certain things we've been doing in a particular way for many years (such as dealing with our anger, for example). We also need to be aware of many subconscious activities, such as behavioral actions that convey wrong impressions.

Helping another person act and respond in an emotionally intelligent way is difficult, for a number of reasons. You deal with a person who is less known to you than you are to yourself. You deal with someone who has not had the opportunity you've had while reading this book to learn how to use emotional intelligence. And there is an added dynamic in the situation, the relationship between you and the other person.

Though extremely difficult, helping others to help themselves is one of the most rewarding practices of emotional intelligence. You help the other person learn, grow, be more productive, and develop a relationship that is characterized by trust and loyalty—two assets not often seen in corporate America. Your payoff is to enjoy the enhanced relationship with the person you help, to learn and grow in the process, and to be perceived as an essential member of the company who knows how to use emotional intelligence. The company benefits from the productiveness resulting from your efforts.

In this chapter we look at four ways you can help others help themselves:

1. Keep your emotional perspective.
2. Know how to calm an out-of-control person.
3. Be a supportive listener.
4. Help with goal planning and goal reaching.

In this chapter we examine how, together, your interpersonal expertise, your ability to help others, and your own emotional intelligence help create the emotionally intelligent organization.

Keep Your Emotional Perspective

In Chapter Two we looked at the many ways you can manage your emotions. What we didn't discuss then, but explore now, is how another person's emotions affect you. Think of going to speak with someone about a slightly touchy subject; let's look again at an example from Chapter Two, Gerald, who doesn't return files. You feel calm and in control when you approach him. But he becomes quite irate with you for mentioning what he considers such a trivial thing, for not recognizing the many things he does for you, and by not understanding his need to hold on to the files. Suddenly you find yourself becoming very angry with him and answering in a hostile tone of voice. What's happening here is that Gerald has infected you with his anger. Many emotions—anger, fear, depression, anxiety, and enthusiasm—can be contagious, spreading from one individual to another. We allow them to spread by subconsciously mimicking certain behaviors in the other person that stem from particular emotions. In this case, Gerald is probably raising his voice, looking at you piercingly, and maybe gesticulating furiously. These behaviors, reflecting his anger, are easily picked up. When you begin mimicking those behaviors, you start experiencing the emotion that is causing them—anger. The anger that you pick up then prevents you from thinking clearly and being able to solve problems.

The good news is that emotional contagion is preventable. Here's what you can do to prevent another person's negative emotions from infecting you:

- Anticipate the other person's emotional state.

- Tune in to the other person's behavior.

- Use instructive statements.

- Use relaxation techniques.

For the most part, these techniques should be familiar to you from earlier chapters.

Anticipate the Other Person's Emotional State

Very often it's not possible to anticipate another person's emotional state, because you just have no clues (when meeting a new client, for example). But in some situations, it is possible. The value in doing so is that you're able to differentiate your emotions from those of the other person and to strategize how to handle the situation most effectively.

Suppose you're meeting with one of your managers, Patrick, to discuss the low morale in his division. It's probably safe to assume that he feels anxious about the meeting, because as a manager he is failing to keep morale at a good level. It's also likely that he feels depressed, because the low morale is affecting him too. By anticipating this, you first recognize that anxiety and depression are *his* emotions, not yours. Try to figure out the best way to conduct the discussion. You can try to relieve Patrick's anxiety by telling him what a good manager he is and how you understand that the extra work his division has been given recently must make it very difficult to maintain high morale. To help alleviate his depression, suggest he look at all the positive contributions his division has made, rather than looking at what they haven't been able to accomplish.

Now let's take a completely different situation. You're about to announce to your workgroup that they are receiving bonuses for the last project they worked on. You know this will cause great glee, and the group may become so excited about this news that they won't be able to listen to the other points you need to discuss in the meeting. So you decide to hold the announcement of the bonus until after all the other business is out of the way.

By anticipating the other person's emotional state, you help guide the outcome in a positive direction, and you enable yourself to control your own emotions so that you are in the right frame of mind for productively dealing with the situation.

Tune in to Your Awareness of Others

In Chapter One, you learned that developing high self-awareness involves tuning in to your senses, getting in touch with your feelings, learning what your intentions are, and paying attention to your actions. By applying what you learned there to another person, you can become aware of what emotion he or she is experiencing. Knowing what emotion you're dealing with is the key to figuring out how best not to "catch" the emotion, because you are then cued to be on the alert for it, and also to be aware if you start mimicking any corresponding behaviors.

Patrick is talking with you about the low morale among your coworkers. He talks slowly, in a low voice, sitting slumped in his chair and looking down at the floor. By turning your awareness way up, you notice that his posture, tone of voice, and facial expressions suggest that he is depressed. You have managed somehow to remain unaffected by the low morale in your group, and you certainly don't want to succumb to it now. By recognizing the emotion Patrick is experiencing, you can then alert yourself to avoid catching it; you can also check whether you too are sitting slumped in a chair, frowning, or exhibiting any other behaviors associated with depression.

Use Instructive Statements

We also discussed instructive statements in Chapter Two, in managing your own emotions. With Patrick, here are examples of instructive statements you might use internally: *Patrick is depressed because of the low morale. Just because he is depressed doesn't mean that I have to be. I won't be infected by his depression. I will be positive.* In Gerald's, you might tell yourself: *Gerald is really angry that I'm speaking with him about this. No matter how angry he gets, I'll remain calm. I'll breathe deeply and speak a little slower than usual.*

These instructive statements help you keep your emotional detachment from the other person, and they also enable you to understand more clearly what he is experiencing and thus act appropriately.

Use Your Relaxation Response

You learned how to use the conditioned relaxation response in Chapter Two. Its purpose is to be able to notice and turn off arousal that, if left unchecked, causes unpleasant emotions to take over, thereby preventing you from thinking and acting effectively. If you feel yourself beginning to catch another person's negative emotion, or you fear that you are susceptible, then use this technique.

■■■

Emotional Intelligence at Work

I was having a casual talk with my boss about my holiday trip. Suddenly I began to feel uncomfortable and ill at ease. I started thinking that I must be boring her, because she was fidgeting and twitching a bit. So I excused myself, saying I had an important phone call to make.

As I got back to my office, I realized that I had felt fine when I started talking with her. What I was telling her was interesting, and she didn't look bored. So then I started asking myself if I could have picked up my discomfort from her. I know she is a shy person who feels uncomfortable being with other people—she's less uncomfortable talking just about the "facts" of work. I realized that the fidgeting and twitching probably weren't related to boredom but discomfort.

The next day I decided to try something different. I said to myself, "OK, she's feeling uncomfortable, so I'll try to put her at her ease." I began by continuing where I had left off, telling her about my trip. But I also said, "I enjoy being able to share this nonwork stuff with you." This seemed to put her at her ease—and me too. (Brendan C., administrative assistant)

■■■

Once you are able to keep your emotional perspective and avoid emotional contagion, you're in a good position to help an out-of-control person regain composure because you can think and perceive clearly.

Know How to Calm an Out-of-Control Person

We want to calm someone out of control because if we don't, we have no hope at all of being able to help that individual. Someone out of control is definitely in need of help, and as an emotionally intelligent person it is your responsibility to assist those in need.

Calming down means reducing the person's emotional arousal. Recall from Chapter Two that one way you can control your own arousal is by using relaxation techniques. You should assume that the relaxation response is unfamiliar to this person and thus try to get the person to slow down. Until the person slows down, rational thoughts or any kind of meaningful discussion is quite impossible. Once he or she slows down, then help redirect the conversation to diminish the arousal level further. Let's discuss in more detail these two ways of calming someone.

Use Slow-Down Techniques

These techniques include whatever you can do or say that enables the other person to stop breathing so fast, moving so quickly, and carrying out any other actions that reflect a heightened state of arousal. One technique that generally backfires is to tell the person to relax or calm down; the usual response is quite the opposite.

Suppose your assistant Margaret comes in, riddled with anxiety. The pressure of the project she is working on is too much for her; she paces frantically around your office, saying over and over, "I just can't do it! It's just too much! This project is never going to get done and then we'll lose the account."

Here are some ways to help her slow down.

■■■

Tips for Helping a Person to Slow Down

1. Suggest that she take a seat. "Let's sit down and talk about this, Margaret." When she stops pacing and does so, she's more in a resting state.

2. Offer something to drink. It can be water or a caffeine-free drink, both of which quite literally help the cool-down process. Drinking something also helps prevent dry mouth, which only makes her feel more anxious if not eliminated.

3. Ask her to speak more slowly. You might say, "I really want to hear what you're saying, Margaret, but I can't when you're talking so

quickly. So could you please speak a little more slowly?" By slow-
ing down her speech, Margaret helps reduce her own arousal.

4. Give her a creative time-out. We saw in Chapter Two how time-
outs can be very effective in defusing a volatile situation by slow-
ing down your emotional responses. Tell Margaret that you need
to run to the bathroom, or put something in the mail, or pass a
quick message on to someone. This gives her a few minutes
alone, during which time she hopefully takes a few deep breaths
and composes herself to a degree.

Once she slows down and has her emotions under some control, you can begin to alter the course of the conversation in a more
productive direction.

■■■

Redirect the Conversation

People who are angry or anxious tend to repeat the same statements
over and over, which only serves to lock them more tightly into
their heightened emotional state. Margaret keeps saying, "I just
can't do it! It's too much!" Even after she sits down and has a drink
of water, her mind may still be repeating the statements. You need
to interrupt and break the cycle by causing her to look at the problem a bit differently. One way you can do this is by offering alternative perspectives.

By getting her to consider alternative perspectives, you help her
look at the situation from a more rational (usually better) view-
point, which then puts you both somewhat closer to a solution. Like
most people who experience anxiety, Margaret is feeling uncertain
about the outcome of her predicament, so she blows it out of pro-
portion, turning it into a catastrophe (the project won't get done,
and you'll lose the account). You might say, "Well, I'm not worried
about it getting done. I know you will be able to do it." You might

also say, "The client isn't going to dump us. They know how difficult this project is." Such comments may jolt Margaret out of her negative ruminations and help her see that perhaps the situation isn't as dire as she thinks.

As you and Margaret talk further, you learn that the real reason for her anxiety is that she thinks she's in over her head: she doesn't believe she's sufficiently up to speed to accomplish the tasks she needs to do. You can offer to get someone to help her along, teaching her what she doesn't know. This helps get Margaret's emotions under control, as well as opening up some possible solutions to her crisis situation. Your response illustrates the next area of helping others: learning to be a supportive listener.

Be a Supportive Listener

We learned in Chapter Four how important dynamic listening is to establishing effective communication. We have seen how dynamic listening means hearing what the other person is really saying, with filters removed and any emotional subtext uncovered. Now we look at listening as a proactive tool for helping others to better understand a difficult situation, feel more positive about their ability to handle it, and feel validated because of having someone's support.

There are two basic steps to being a supportive listener: acknowledging your acceptance of what the speaker is saying; and helping the speaker clarify thoughts, feelings, and ideas.

Acknowledge Your Acceptance of What the Speaker Is Saying

A person who comes to you in a heightened emotional state already feels vulnerable and probably has a lot of self-doubt. By accepting what the person says without judging or criticizing it, you enable the person to feel secure and safe in discussing what the real issues are (Margaret's fear that she is not sufficiently experienced to complete the project, for example).

Acceptance doesn't necessarily signify agreement, but simple receipt of the message communicated. Following Margaret's outburst, you might say, "I can see how difficult this is for you," or "I can hear how overwhelming this project is for you." You convey to her that you understand and respect the thoughts and feelings she is communicating, and that you are judging neither her nor what she is saying. You can acknowledge acceptance in a number of other ways that are less formal and perhaps feel more comfortable: by nodding your head, smiling, or making short comments such as "I see," "Yes, that's important to you," or "Go on."

It's easy to recognize how such acceptance can encourage the other person to pursue the matter at hand openly and forthrightly. This then gives you valuable data—information about what's really going on in this situation—that you can later use in the problem-solving stage.

If, by contrast, you say to Margaret, "That's ridiculous. This project isn't going to fall apart because of you," she might feel you don't understand what is going on, don't care about what she's feeling, and are rejecting her perception of the situation. Feeling more vulnerable than ever, most likely she will not continue the discussion and her anxiety will remain at the same intense level, or perhaps even rise.

Acknowledging your acceptance of what a distressed person shares with you is a good application of your interpersonal expertise because it reflects your sensitivity to the other person's vulnerability. Your use of sensitivity then helps you establish a connection, and it becomes the basis for a mutual discovery of how to resolve the situation effectively.

One tip to keep in mind: if your internal thoughts show that you are judging or blaming the other person (*Margaret always feels overwhelmed* or *Her insecurity is certainly going to undermine this project*), you need to recognize that you are not listening with acceptance. Try having internal thoughts like this: *I respect Margaret's thoughts and feelings. I will listen without making any value judgments. I accept the validity for her of what she is saying.*

Once you acknowledge your acceptance of the person's thoughts and feelings, you are ready to move on to helping the other person clarify those thoughts and feelings.

Help the Speaker to Clarify Thoughts, Feelings, and Ideas

As we become distressed, our thinking becomes distorted ("We'll lose the account") and our feelings, being so all-consuming, lose their identity (Margaret's anxiety appears as anger over the situation, but it's really about fear of being inadequate). Until our thoughts and feelings become clear to us, we can't use the information they give us meaningfully; thus we have little hope of working through the distressful situation.

We saw in Chapter One how self-awareness is about recognizing, getting in touch with, and understanding our thoughts, feelings, and ideas (along with our actions, intentions, and appraisals, which are not the focus in this section). In the context of interpersonal expertise, you help others become more self-aware through encouraging them to be more precise in what they wish to convey. You help them clarify their thoughts, feelings, and ideas.

In helping others with clarification, you must always keep in mind that your role is to draw out their thoughts and feelings, not to impose your own. You may become impatient trying, for example, to help Margaret see why she believes she won't be able to complete the project. Instead of using clarification tools (which I introduce in a moment), we blurt out what we think and feel about the case at hand: "You're way off base here, Margaret. The project isn't impossible. You just need to get some help learning how to do all the tasks." In thrusting our insights on others, we invalidate their own thoughts and feelings and deny them the opportunity of reaching their own understanding. It is helpful to keep this in mind as you read through the next section.

To help others clarify their thoughts and feelings, you can (1) repeat what the person says, (2) paraphrase what you think the person really means, (3) share your perceptions of the situation, and (4) ask purposeful questions.

Repeat What the Other Person Says

People sometimes don't mean what they say, especially in times of intense emotionality. This may be because they exaggerate, use vague generalities that give the wrong impression, or in the heat of the moment forget to turn on the censor. By repeating what they say, you enable them to hear it in a way that often causes them to revise as they recognize that the words don't accurately convey what they really mean.

Peter is an irate employee who speaks to you about his coworker, Janice. In the first dialogue below, you fail to use your emotional intelligence; in the second example, you do use it.

> PETER: I can't stand working with Janice anymore. She never gets her work done on time.
> YOU: You don't really mean you can't stand Janice. She's worked hard on a lot of projects.
> PETER: I'm telling you, I always have to pick up the slack, and that means I have twice as much work to do.
> YOU: Oh, come on now, you're exaggerating.
> PETER: No I'm not. No one ever notices, and she always gets away with it.
> YOU: That's not fair of you to say that.

Now notice the difference when your interpersonal expertise is at work and you repeat what Peter says:

> PETER: I can't stand working with Janice anymore. She never gets her work done on time.
> YOU: You can't stand working with Janice because she never gets her work done on time.
> PETER: Well, not *never*, but lately it seems to be more often than not. I have to pick up the slack, and that means I have twice as much work to do.

You: You have to pick up the slack, which means you have twice as much work to do.

Peter: I don't *always* pick up the slack. It's not like someone tells me I have to do it, I just feel like I should do it. And no one ever notices.

You: No one ever notices that Janice doesn't carry her load.

Peter: Maybe they do, but what I mean is no one notices how much work I do.

You can see from these two examples how by repeating what Peter says you enable him to temper his exaggerations and be more specific. By so doing, and by revising much of his wording, he gets at what his real concern is: he is unhappy that he isn't getting recognized for the hard work he does. His anger and frustration don't have to do so much with Janice not carrying through on her tasks, but with his not getting praise or appreciation. In this case, as his manager you also learn something useful: that you need to be more forthcoming with your recognition of Peter's hard work.

Repetition serves another important function here: it acknowledges the legitimacy of Peter's anger, frustration, and concern about his unjust treatment. The question of whether or not he is "right" is not the issue here, because you are not passing judgment.

If you look again at the first example, you can see a few things. First of all, at the end of the discussion, Peter's anger does not seem to abate but perhaps is even increasing. There is good reason for that: you fail to help him understand what he is really trying to say; you dismiss his concern about the unfairness of the situation and deny the legitimacy of his feelings; and by challenging him, you leave him feeling defensive, which only makes the futility of his situation more apparent. Unlike the second dialogue, in which you use your interpersonal expertise, in the first instance you fail to learn anything from the encounter that can help you do your job better.

A word of caution: when you repeat what someone has said, it can sometimes be interpreted by the other person as being patronizing.

You need to take special care that neither the tone of your voice nor your facial expression suggests that you are patronizing. Instead, imply that the reason you are repeating the other person's statements is to facilitate understanding.

Paraphrase What You Think the Person Really Means

Paraphrasing is another way to help others clarify their thoughts, feelings, and ideas. It's a little more proactive than repeating what someone says because you must first take into consideration the actual words and what the person is really trying to say with them, the emotional subtext of what the individual is saying, and nonverbal clues. Then you must put that information together and restate, in your own words, what you believe the person really wants you to take away from the conversation. Although paraphrasing does not include making a value judgment of what the person says, it necessitates a judgment regarding what seems to be important to the speaker.

Paraphrasing also requires that you sometimes go out on a limb. As we've learned, people often say things in such a way that the meaning is incomprehensible and elusive. But you need to make an effort to synthesize the meaning, and sometimes you are mistaken. But even your error helps the other person realize that the meaning isn't clear. On the other hand, if you repeatedly don't seem to catch the meaning of what someone is trying to communicate, then the other person may conclude that the fault is with you, that you don't know how to listen effectively.

As you can see, paraphrasing draws on many of your emotional intelligence skills: awareness, perceptiveness, self-disclosure, dynamic listening. Take Peter the angry employee. Here's how you might paraphrase what he says:

PETER: I can't stand working with Janice anymore. She never gets her work done on time. I have to pick up the slack, and that means I have twice as much work to do.

YOU: I see. What you're saying is you're feeling overwhelmed with the amount of work you have to do and feel rather put upon because you don't believe Janice is doing her share.

PETER: Well, I wouldn't say *put upon* because it's not like someone is telling me I *have* to do it. I just feel like I should do it.

YOU: So you feel an obligation to the department to make sure that even if someone is not doing her share, you'll see the project through, and that seems quite a burden to you.

PETER: That's part of it. It's also that I don't think anyone notices.

YOU: You're feeling upset and hurt because here you are doing all this extra work and no one is giving you any recognition.

PETER: Yes, that's right.

You can see from this example how paraphrasing helps both you and Peter to get at what is truly bothering him. You can also see that this is an interactive process. Peter gives you some information, you interpret it and give it back to him somewhat revised, he then revises your revision and adds something new, and so on, until you arrive at the real meaning of his conversation.

Share Your Perceptions of the Other Person's Feelings

We see in the preceding two sections how repeating what another person says or paraphrasing it brings you quite close to uncovering the thoughts, ideas, and feelings that are the real issue. Here we learn how to focus just on the feelings, getting to them through observing both verbal and nonverbal behaviors. We then deduce from those behaviors the feelings that the person is experiencing and expressing or attempting to express.

Let's say Peter comes to you with his same problem:

PETER (walking back and forth in your office, talking quickly and loudly, gesticulating a bit wildly with his arms): I can't stand working with Janice anymore. She never gets her work done on time.

YOU: You seem angry about it.

PETER: Well, actually I'm mostly frustrated because I have to pick up the slack, and that means I have twice as much work to do.

YOU: I can hear your frustration, but I'm also picking up that you're mad.

PETER: I am because it's just not fair that Janice gets away without doing her job. (He sits, looking down at the floor, talking slowly.) And no one notices how much work I do to make sure the department doesn't fall behind.

YOU: It sounds like you're pretty sad and hurt about not getting recognition.

PETER: I am.

You can see how the clues from Peter's behavior help you determine the emotions he is experiencing. The loud, wild behavior he exhibits when he first comes into your office suggests anger. When he takes a seat, his downcast behavior suggests sadness and hurt. Here, too, you can also see that the back-and-forth dialogue enables you both to get closer to what emotions are operating here.

The reason for sharing your perceptions of the other person's feelings is twofold. First, as you can see here, your appraisals of Peter's feelings provide him with another way of viewing his situation. He really isn't aware, until you help him draw it out, that what's causing him to feel so upset is the lack of recognition for all his hard work. Second, you get feedback on your perceptions, which means you can revise them accordingly, which then determines your subsequent course of action. If, instead of sadness and hurt, anger is really the driving emotion, then you certainly want to talk with Janice about doing more work, or maybe even get someone else in to help out.

As is the case with the practice of so many emotional intelligence skills, you must use sensitivity here. Although it's important to share and check your perceptions of another person's feelings, you can do more harm through insensitivity than by neglecting to discuss your perceptions. Here are some ways you can learn to use sensitivity in sharing your perceptions.

■■■

Tips for Effectively Sharing Your Perceptions of Another Person's Feelings

1. Avoid implying that you are making a judgment. Rather, be very clear that the perceptions are yours and yours alone.

2. Avoid suggesting that you are making a negative evaluation. Be sure that your vocal inflection, facial expression, and word emphasis all suggest acceptance of what the other person is saying.

3. Avoid challenging statements. "You sure seem out of it" is going to cause the other person to become defensive, whereas "I have the impression that you're upset" isn't. Similarly with "You still don't understand" instead of "I seem to be confusing you"; or "You're getting uptight" instead of "This conversation is rather difficult."

4. Repeatedly verify the accuracy of your perceptions. Ask the other person if you are correctly picking up on the feeling being conveyed: "I sense that you're feeling frustrated. Would you say this is true?"

■■■

Ask Purposeful Questions

Asking purposeful questions helps the other person clarify thoughts and feelings; it also helps you gain better understanding of the situation at hand. The more specific your question is, the more likely you are to direct the thinking, and consequently the answers, of the other person in a way that is useful to both of you.

There are three levels of purposeful questions: open-ended, directed, and specific. The emotionally intelligent way of using these three levels of questioning is usually to start with the general and move to the specific. That way you enable the other person to feel comfortable revealing information as you go, proceeding deeper into the sources of the problem. Asking a specific question too early can sometimes cause the other person to go on guard and respond defensively.

To explore how you can use these three levels of questioning, let's look at a dilemma your coworker Carla is facing. She has been offered an overseas assignment and doesn't know whether or not to accept it. She comes to you to discuss the pros and cons.

CARLA: The overseas position is exciting, and there would be a pay increase, but I'm not sure I know enough about it. I'd be moving away from Nathan, and I see that hurting our relationship. It occurs to me that I'm using the opportunity of going overseas to get away from the politics around here. But I don't want that to be a reason to take this new position. Plus, who knows what problems there will be with this new position. I'm so confused.

YOU: It does indeed sound like a very complicated situation. [This shows acceptance of the situation and Carla's confusion.] What are your thoughts about it? [You start with an open-ended question.]

CARLA: I think I'm really ready for something new, but I'm afraid I might be disappointed and end up not liking the new situation as much as my current one.

YOU: I can see that. A major change can certainly cause you to be anxious. [Acceptance of her feelings] What do you see as the pros and cons of the overseas position? [Directed question]

CARLA: I think I would be very happy living in London for a while, but I love Nathan a lot and wouldn't want to break up with him as a result. I'll be making more money, but I think I'll also be spending more money because it costs a lot to live in London. I've been unhappy with all the political infighting and competition around here, but then I don't know whether I'll be better off over there, and it makes me very anxious to consider such a big move with so little information.

YOU: What information do you think you need about the new job to be in a better position to make your decision? [Specific question]

CARLA: Well, I'd like to know what the work environment is like in the company over there—is it very structured or fairly loose, do people tend to work competitively or collaboratively? I would like to have a sense of how much it would cost me to live there more or less the way I'm living here, so I can see if the salary differential is significant. I'd like to have some more details about what exactly I would be doing and who I would be working with. And I guess I'd also like to know about employment opportunities in London in Nathan's field, in case he decides he might like to move, too.

You begin the conversation by assuming nothing about Carla's concerns or what her real issues are. Instead, you ask a general question that leads her to convey to you some of her feelings, namely her anxiety about making such a major change in her life. By letting her define the issues, you leave the door open for her to talk more revealingly, which helps her look more closely at what she might like and not like about the new position. From there, you discover what is probably the major issue for her—not knowing enough about the new position—and lead her to come up with a list of some very specific questions to which she would like answers. Carla is now in a position to go get the answers and come closer to resolving whether or not she should accept the assignment.

A cautionary word: you need to be very careful not to ask a question in such a way that it doesn't solicit the other person's point of view but rather expresses your own. Suppose that when Carla mentions the political infighting you ask, "Do you think that your disgust with the politics of the place really has more to do with your being upset that others have gotten positions you wanted?" You are offering your own conclusion here and in so doing are making Carla feel judged. Not only that, but assuming your conclusion is wrong, you place her in the position of having to defend herself rather than being able to clarify her situation.

If you find that your questions are an attempt to convince the other person to accept your ideas, then you are focusing on your own intentions, desires, and interpretations. You're losing sight of what your role in the situation is meant to be: a guide, helping the person gain understanding of a difficult situation.

We've looked at four ways you can help others clarify their thoughts and feelings: repeating what they say, paraphrasing it, sharing your perceptions of the situation, and asking purposeful questions. You can use these techniques in short encounters as well as in lengthy conversations. Even though you may at first feel clumsy or awkward, with more practice you should feel quite comfortable, using them naturally and effectively.

Guiding others to help clarify their thoughts and feelings enables you to take satisfaction in helping them help themselves; at the same time, it allows others to perceive you as a person with good interpersonal expertise. In the next section, we look at another way to do that: by helping others to plan and reach their goals.

Helping Others Plan Their Goals and Reach Them

As we've seen in this chapter, helping others help themselves generally involves helping others sort through a problem. In the last section, we learned how by being a supportive listener you help others better understand the situation that is causing them distress. The next step is for them to take a course of action that resolves the situation favorably. This is where you come in again: you help others set goals and then help them reach those goals. You might be called upon by a coworker who wants to build up a client base, or by a colleague facing a major dilemma (such as Carla, who must decide whether or not she should transfer to London).

There are three tacks you can take to help others with goal planning and goal reaching: (1) help the person draw up a contract, (2) use role playing and modeling, and (3) reinforce positive steps. These three techniques can be used individually, but it is often effective to use them in conjunction, with each increasing the effectiveness of the others.

Help the Person Draw up a Contract

A contract is an agreement between two parties, in this case, between you and the person you are helping. As part of the contract, the other person agrees to carry out or attempt to carry out a particular task and then report the results back to you. The person has already decided on a course of action; the contract serves as a motivational tool to help ensure that the task gets done.

The contract may be stated verbally or in writing, though it is my experience that a written contract is preferable because it leaves no room for misunderstanding. Implicit in the contract is acknowledgment that the problem belongs to the other person; in exchange for the time and energy you devote to helping resolve the problem, the other person promises to perform the steps necessary to reach the goal.

Because of the formal nature of a contract and the effort involved in drawing it up and following it, generally you should suggest using one only with a major goal, such as moving to a different division. Don't suggest a contract if, for example, a person needs to be motivated to write a five-page report.

A contract must include:

- Definition of the goal

- A list of the steps necessary to accomplish the goal

- Commitment from the other person to follow through on those steps

- Commitment from you to provide support, encouragement, and assistance in defining action steps as needed

Carla's goal might be to find out as much as she can about the overseas position. The steps she takes can include identifying and talking with someone who has worked there; speaking with people who currently work there about her specific position; talking with someone who lives in London to see how the cost of living compares to that where she lives; and making initial inquiries in Nathan's field about job possibilities in London.

When the actions have been taken (or not taken), Carla reports to you that they were or were not completed. She might tell you that she spoke with someone who worked for the overseas company, and she now has a better sense of the kind of place it is. She spoke with three employees at the company, including her prospective manager, about details of the position. She called a few people she knows who live in London to get a sense of the cost of living. But she hasn't been able to find out about job possibilities for Nathan.

Although many of the steps may be uncomfortable for Carla to take, she is motivated by the existence of the contract: you and she have an agreement, and she needs to fulfill her obligations, just as you do. The satisfaction she experiences as she carries out each step and reports to you on her success further fuels her motivation.

Use Modeling and Role Playing

Many times, after an action has been decided upon, the other person still finds it nearly impossible to perform the action. The reason is that the action is often unfamiliar and therefore causes anxiety, which effectively prevents the person from taking action. You can help here, first of all, by demonstrating how the action might be performed: whether it's criticizing a boss, making a presentation, firing someone, taking a controversial stand in a team meeting, or any other potentially anxiety-producing or fear-producing action. Second, you can engage in a mock dialogue with the other person, in which you play the part of the other person and the other person assumes the part of the boss or soon-to-be-fired employee, and then switch roles.

The first technique is called modeling: you demonstrate to the other person effective behaviors and responses to be used in a particular situation, or even ineffective ones that it's best not to use. The second technique is called role playing, whereby you enable the other person both to observe you modeling (when you play the part of that person) and to explore through live interaction how she might act in the real situation when she plays herself. This gives her the opportunity to find out what works and what doesn't, and to rehearse a discomforting encounter so that it feels less uncomfortable and has a better chance of being resolved satisfactorily. Modeling can be practiced on its own, but role playing always involves modeling. Together they allow you to help an individual develop and practice new skills that are necessary to perform a particular task, and to develop the confidence needed to undertake the task and follow through with it.

Let's go back to Carla. Suppose she just can't seem to make the call to one of the employees at the overseas firm to discuss what the company culture is like, what the other employees are like. Carla has never made such a call before, and it seems to be rather threatening: if she makes a bad impression or asks the wrong questions, she may end up having the job offer rescinded. You can model for her the best ways she might carry out the conversation, or you can engage in role playing. You first take her part, so she can see how you would approach this other person initially, draw the person out, and get useful answers.

Then you switch roles, with Carla playing herself and you playing the employee in London. Through your responses, you show Carla what's a good question and what isn't. For example, if she asks, "Is it a fun place to work?" you might reply, "Well, it isn't Disneyland." Be sure to let her know that your response is meant to suggest that you don't feel it's a question likely to elicit a useful answer, or one that will put Carla in a good position (explain that the other person might hear her question as revealing her to be frivolous). On the other hand, if Carla asks, "Would you say the members of your team work collaboratively?" you might respond, "We do on many projects, and we use problem solving a lot for one another on other projects, but mostly we work individually." Again, tell Carla that this may not be fact; you have no idea what the work environment in the London office is like, and you have fabricated the response. The point is you want Carla to know that her question is a good one, one that might give her some useful information that can help her make her decision as to whether or not she should accept the job offer.

In spite of mastering the role-playing situation, a person could fail to use the effective responses and behaviors in the real situation. Although modeling and role playing give others the skills to succeed and the confidence and belief that they will succeed, sometimes in the real situation anxiety overtakes them and they can't perform as well as they might otherwise. To help prevent this from happening, use your emotional intelligence skill of recognizing and appraising the underlying feelings brought up by the situation (uncovered during the role playing), and then discuss them.

Let's say that as Carla plays herself during role playing, her voice begins to quiver, she stutters a bit, and talks hesitantly. You might say, "Sounds like you feel anxious when you ask that question. Is this the case?" Then encourage her to talk about her anxiety. She says she is worried about the outcome of the call and feels so much depends upon it. Acknowledge that her anxiety is perfectly understandable, and reassure her that through practice she can ensure the success of the call. If she still seems anxious, you can suggest she use any of the techniques for managing emotions that we discussed in Chapter Two, such as engaging in a constructive internal dialogue or using relaxation. You can also engage in last-minute mini-role plays that address the anxiety underlying the situation. For example, just before Carla makes the call to London, you might role-play part of the conversation she is about to have in which she inquires about vacation days.

The main purpose of modeling and role playing is, of course, to help others be able to take productive actions so they can reach their goals. The underlying purpose goes beyond just teaching appropriate responses for particular situations: you want to help others by encouraging confidence in their ability to handle similar distressful situations, and by teaching them emotional management skills to help toward that end. Here are some ways that you can use modeling and role playing effectively.

■■■

Tips for Using Modeling and Role Playing Effectively

1. Ask yourself if you can be an effective model. There may very well be situations where you can't be. If you are the unassertive type, you may have difficulty demonstrating to another person how to confront his boss about her abrasive behavior. You might say the words, but, lacking conviction, be perceived as not credible or realistic. If you determine that you can't effectively model the required behavior, consider who else might be an effective model, and then check with that person about being available to the individual for role play.

2. Show enthusiasm. How you model is as important as what you model. As the person catches on to your modeling and demonstrates effective responses, show enthusiasm. He or she is likely to pick up the emotion, which works as motivational arousal. Let's say you're playing the person Carla is going to talk with in London, and she's playing herself. After she asks you a number of questions, you (in your role) say, "Those were really interesting questions. You seem eager to come work here, but also very deliberate in making your decision." Look enthusiastic as you say this. By doing so, you inspire her to want to have this discussion with the real person.

3. Consider realistically the person and the situation. Suppose Thomas, who has come to you for help in confronting an abrasive boss, is a nonassertive person. Your appraisal of what he is like and the nature of the situation he faces tells you that no

amount of role playing will give him the skills or confidence he needs to resolve the situation effectively. You might suggest an alternative plan: writing to his boss, explaining that he has difficulty with a face-to-face discussion of such a delicate subject.

4. Structure the modeling session so that total failure is nearly impossible. Remember that building confidence is one of your goals here. So even if the person's first attempt at practicing responses to a situation has negative consequences, praise what is done correctly: "Your body posture and body language really convey your earnestness." Then use productive criticism (discussed in Chapter Four) to help the person improve next time: "The loudness of your voice suggests anger, and if your boss senses your anger, she may dismiss what you're trying to convey to her. So it would be much better if you spoke more slowly and quietly." If there is almost nothing positive you can say to the person, then at least recognize the person's willingness to try role playing, and suggest more practice.

■■■

Emotional Intelligence at Work

Part of my job as a vocational counselor at a Veterans Administration hospital is to help patients find jobs in the community. Many of them are very anxious about the job interview, especially when they are asked where they live. They get very embarrassed when they have to say they live at the hospital. Since they know they are going to have to answer that question, they rarely go for job interviews.

I have found a tool that really helps: I role-play the interview with them. I play the role of the job interviewer and I ask them all sorts of questions, including, of course, where they are living. When they say a hospital, I say, "My god, what's wrong with you?" I really make it difficult. If they have trouble, we stop the role play and discuss their options. Sometimes I switch roles and demonstrate how they can respond. And I make sure I give them plenty of praise for doing things well. I find this gives them confidence.

This becomes a very good learning experience, and not just for them. By playing their role, I find I gain a better awareness of just how stressful the job interview can be for them. (Malcolm S., vocational counselor)

■■■

We look next at the third way to help others set and plan their goals: reinforcing their positive steps.

Reinforce Positive Steps

After you get a commitment from someone to carry out certain actions necessary to reach a designated goal, and you help the person practice the behaviors necessary to perform those actions successfully, the next way you can help bring the goal closer is to reinforce positive steps. By giving praise and rewards, you help motivate productive action.

Like drawing up a contract with another person, reinforcement is a very effective way to motivate someone who already wishes to take certain action. It's also a good motivational tool for those who become easily distracted from a task at hand and need some encouragement to get back on track. By reinforcing certain behavior, you encourage the person to repeat the behavior, in the desire to get more praise. In the context of interpersonal expertise, you not only offer reinforcement to others but you help them learn how to reinforce themselves, independently of you.

Suppose you feel that nonassertive Thomas could actually learn to confront his boss about her abrasiveness. Let's say you try role playing but it isn't sufficiently successful; Thomas isn't ready yet to have a productive talk with his boss. During the modeling part of role playing, you demonstrate assertive behavior to Thomas, so at least he knows what it is. Your role, in helping him to help himself, is to praise him every time you see him exhibiting behavior that might loosely be called assertive. Let's refer back to this case as we learn some ways to use productive reinforcement.

■■■

Tips for Using Reinforcement Effectively

1. Be consistent. Reinforcement is much more effective when it is practiced consistently. Reward Thomas when he offers an opinion in the meeting ("Thomas, that was great use of your assertiveness"), when he asks to cut in line and photocopy a few pages instead of waiting for the publicity manager to copy hundreds of her packets ("You're really learning to be assertive, Thomas. That's great"), and every time that you witness his assertiveness. Haphazard reinforcement, in which behavior is sometimes rewarded and sometimes not, is much less effective. The goal is for Thomas to associate practicing the behavior pattern with a positive outcome.

2. Reward the behavior as soon as possible after it is manifested. Every minute or event that separates the behavior from the reward lessens the power of the reward, so try to reduce to a minimum the intervening events. Give Thomas a thumbs-up sign in the meeting after he uses assertiveness, or at the very least go up to him and praise him immediately after the meeting.

3. Define the cause-and-effect relationship. For reinforcement to work, Thomas must understand the relationship between practicing the behavior and being rewarded. He needs to know that every time he uses assertiveness you will smile at him and say something positive: "It's great to see you using your assertiveness." "You're really catching on about how to use your assertiveness."

4. Be sure that the reinforcement is meaningful. If the reward isn't meaningful or desirable, the person is going to be much less motivated to use a particular behavior or get a certain task done. Praise from you, his respected colleague, is sufficient reinforcement. In the case of boring, repetitive tasks, it is especially important that the reinforcement be desirable. Recall Jonette, the sales manager in Chapter Three, who uses emotional intelligence at work to put on music whenever her employees have to do their

tedious paperwork, as that helps them enjoy the process and they get their paperwork done in even less time than usual. The music here may be considered both a motivator (the pulsing rhythms get endorphins going and the arousal level up) and also reinforcement (it's a reward for the boring paperwork the employees must do).

■■■

Because you want others to be able to reinforce their own behaviors or actions so they can be independent, you need to encourage them to come up with a suitable reinforcement plan. Let's return to Carla. Suppose she decides that after each call to London and each question session regarding the overseas assignment with someone in her current company, she will reward herself by having internal thoughts containing much praise ("I'm really doing well with these calls"; "I'm showing a lot of self-confidence") and by reading a few pages from her guidebook on London. The rewards she has planned for herself make her feel so good that she looks forward to getting them, but she knows that to get them she must carry out her distressful task. Rewarding herself, she motivates herself.

By contracting with others, using role playing with them, and giving them reinforcement, you help motivate them. In the process, you help them motivate themselves; you give them the necessary confidence, skills, and tools so that eventually they take action and accomplish goals independently of you.

You have probably noticed that the title of this chapter is "Helping Others Help Themselves." It's not called simply "Helping Others," for a good reason: the whole purpose of the helping we discuss here is to guide others to learn to use their emotional intelligence so that they can help themselves be more productive, effective, and successful. Once they become adept at using their emotional intelligence, they then help others help themselves by learning to use their emotional intelligence. We're striving for *the emotionally intelligent organization*, one in which all employees use their emotional intelligence to the fullest.

Moving Toward the Emotionally Intelligent Organization

At the very beginning of this chapter, we said a work organization is an integrated system that depends upon the performance of each individual who is a part of it and on the interrelationship of the individuals. Throughout the book, we've seen the value of using our emotional intelligence both in how we conduct ourselves and in how we relate to others. This is all building toward—and we should all be striving for—the emotionally intelligent organization, a company in which the employees create a culture that continuously applies the skills and tools of emotional intelligence.

In such a workplace, all employees take responsibility for increasing their own emotional intelligence through developing high self-awareness, managing their emotions, and motivating themselves. They each take responsibility for using their emotional intelligence in their relations with others through developing effective communication skills and interpersonal expertise, and through helping others help themselves. And they all take responsibility for using their emotional intelligence to apply all of these improvements to the organization as a whole.

The emotionally intelligent *organization* is much too broad a subject to explore adequately here; that requires a whole book. I raise the topic so you know where your emotional intelligence can take you. Imagine what it might be like to work in a company where, for example, everyone communicates with understanding and respect, where people set group goals and help others to work toward them, and where enthusiasm and confidence in the organization are widespread. As you know by now, emotional intelligence in your organization starts with you. As you practice employing your emotions to enhance your own work performance and work relationships, I challenge you not only to encourage but to inspire the development of emotional intelligence among all the employees in your company. The message is clear: the potential for both individual and organizational success is significant—with the added bonus that it is truly attainable.

Appendix

Developing Your
Emotional Intelligence

This instrument, "Developing Your Emotional Intelligence," is designed to help you gain awareness of your abilities in terms of emotional intelligence and then to help you develop these abilities. The instrument consists of three parts.

Part One requires you to rate your ability to apply emotional intelligence.

Part Two requires you to examine your responses in Part One, looking for strengths and for areas that can be improved.

Part Three requires you to practice and observe your skills in applying emotional intelligence for four weeks. Then you retake Parts One and Two, noting differences from your earlier responses.

Part One

For each item, rate how well you are able to display the ability described. Before responding, try to think of actual situations in which you have been called on to use the ability.

Low ability   **High ability**

1   2   3   4   5   6   7

1. Identify changes in physiological arousal   _____
2. Relax when under pressure in situations   _____
3. Act productively when angry   _____
4. Act productively in situations that arouse anxiety   _____
5. Calm yourself quickly when angry   _____
6. Associate different physical cues with different emotions   _____
7. Use internal "talk" to affect your emotional states   _____
8. Communicate your feelings effectively   _____
9. Reflect on negative feelings without being distressed   _____
10. Stay calm when you are the target of anger from others   _____
11. Know when you are thinking negatively   _____
12. Know when your "self-talk" is instructional   _____
13. Know when you are becoming angry   _____
14. Know how you interpret events you encounter   _____
15. Know what senses you are currently using   _____
16. Accurately communicate what you experience   _____
17. Identify what information influences your interpretations   _____
18. Identify when you experience mood shifts   _____
19. Know when you become defensive   _____
20. Know the impact that your behavior has on others   _____

Low ability   **High ability**

| 1 | 2 | 3 | 4 | 5 | 6 | 7 |

21. Know when you communicate incongruently _____

22. "Gear up" at will _____

23. Regroup quickly after a setback _____

24. Complete long-term tasks in designated time frames _____

25. Produce high energy when doing uninteresting work _____

26. Stop or change ineffective habits _____

27. Develop new and more productive patterns
    of behavior _____

28. Follow words with actions _____

29. Work out conflicts _____

30. Develop consensus with others _____

31. Mediate conflict between others _____

32. Exhibit effective interpersonal communication skills _____

33. Articulate the thoughts of a group _____

34. Influence others, directly or indirectly _____

35. Build trust with others _____

36. Build support teams _____

37. Make others feel good _____

38. Provide advice and support to others, as needed _____

39. Accurately reflect people's feelings back to them _____

40. Recognize when others are distressed _____

41. Help others manage their emotions _____

42. Show empathy to others _____

43. Engage in intimate conversations with others _____

44. Help a group to manage emotions _____

45. Detect incongruence between others' emotions _____
    or feelings and their behaviors

Part Two

Review your responses. The following charts indicate which items reflect which competencies.

Intrapersonal

Self-Awareness	Managing Emotions	Self-Motivation
1, 6, 11, 12, 13, 14, 15, 17, 18, 19, 20, 21	1, 2, 3, 4, 5, 7, 9, 10, 13, 27	7, 22, 23, 25, 26, 27, 28

Interpersonal

Relating Well	Emotional Mentoring
8, 10, 16, 19, 20, 29, 30, 31, 32, 33, 34, 35, 36, 37, 38, 39, 42, 43, 44, 45	8, 10, 16, 18, 34, 35, 37, 38, 39, 40, 41, 44, 45

Organize your responses as follows. For each of the five competencies, count the number of responses for which you scored 4 or lower using tic marks in the *left* column. Count the number of responses for which you scored 5 or higher using tic marks in the *right* column.

Intrapersonal

Competency	Responses of 4 and lower	Responses of 5 and higher
Self-Awareness		
Managing Emotions		
Self-Motivation		

Interpersonal

Competency	Responses of 4 and lower	Responses of 5 and higher
Relating Well		
Emotional Mentoring		

Study your patterns and identify which competencies you want to improve.

Part Three

Based on your response pattern, identify two emotional intelligence competencies that you wish to focus on improving:

1. _____

2. _____

Now identify some specific tasks that will help you master these two competencies of emotional intelligence:

_____

_____

_____

_____

During the next four weeks, practice using your emotional intelligence abilities.

Then retake Parts One and Two. Note differences. Repeat the procedure until your response is 5 or above on all of the items in Part One.

Bibliography

Goleman, D. *Emotional Intelligence*. New York: Bantam, 1995.

Mayer, J. D., and Geher, G. "Emotional Intelligence and the Identification of Emotion." *Intelligence*, 1996, *22*, 89–113.

Mayer, J. D., and Salovey, P. "The Intelligence of Emotional Intelligence." *Intelligence*, 1993, *17*(4), 433–442.

Mayer, J. D., and Salovey, P. "Emotional Intelligence and the Construction and Regulation of Feelings." *Applied and Preventive Psychology*, 1995, *4*, 197–208.

Mayer, J. D., and Salovey, P. "What Is Emotional Intelligence?" In P. Salovey and D. Sluyter (eds.), *Emotional Development and Emotional Intelligence: Implications for Educators*. New York: Basic Books, 1997.

Mayer, J. D., Salovey, P., and Caruso, D. *Emotional IQ Test*. CD-ROM version. Richard Viard (producer). Needham, Mass.: Virtual Entertainment, 1997.

Miller, S., and Nunnally, E. *Alive and Awake*. Minneapolis: Interpersonal Communication Programs, 1975.

Safran, J., and Greenberg, L. *Emotion, Psychotherapy, and Change*. New York: Guilford Press, 1991.

Thayer, R. *The Origin of Everyday Moods*. New York: Oxford University Press, 1996.

Weisinger, H. *Anger at Work*. New York: Morrow, 1995.